EASY PIANO

HEART OF *America*

ISBN 0-634-05364-7

HAL•LEONARD® CORPORATION

7777 W. BLUEMOUND RD. P.O. BOX 13819 MILWAUKEE, WI 53213

Visit Hal Leonard Online at
www.halleonard.com

Contents

AMAZED

Words and Music by MARV GREEN,
CHRIS LINDSEY and AIMEE MAYO

Moderately slow Country Ballad

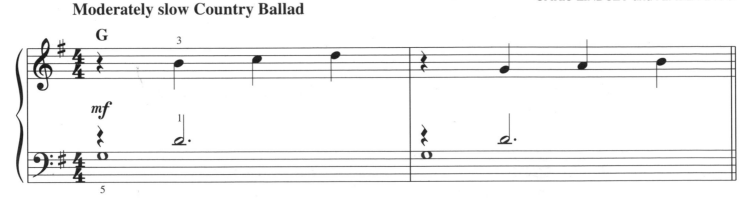

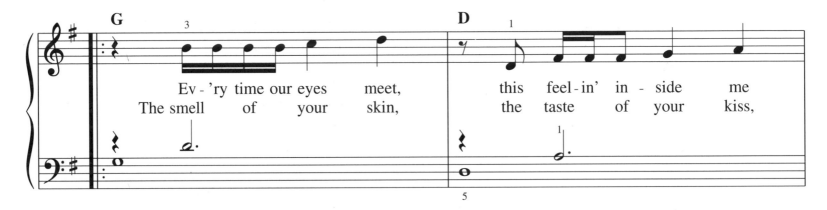

Ev - 'ry time our eyes   meet,   this feel-in' in - side   me
The smell   of   your   skin,   the   taste   of   your   kiss,

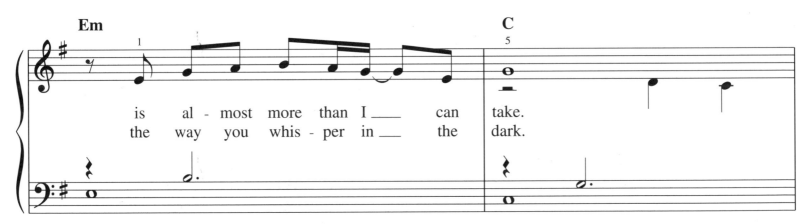

is   al - most more than I ___ can   take.
the   way   you   whis - per in ___ the   dark.

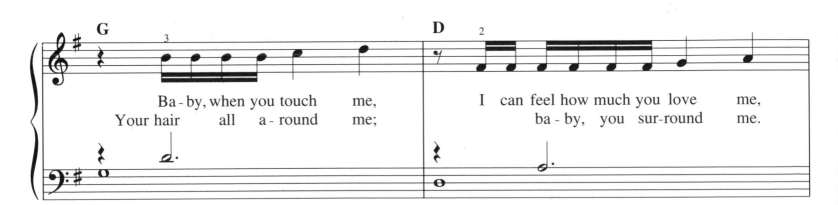

Ba - by, when you touch   me,   I   can feel how much you love   me,
Your hair   all a - round   me;   ba - by,   you sur-round   me.

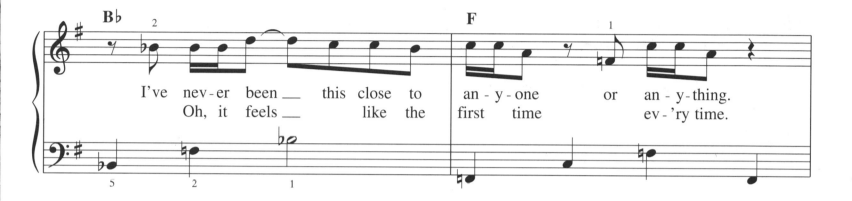

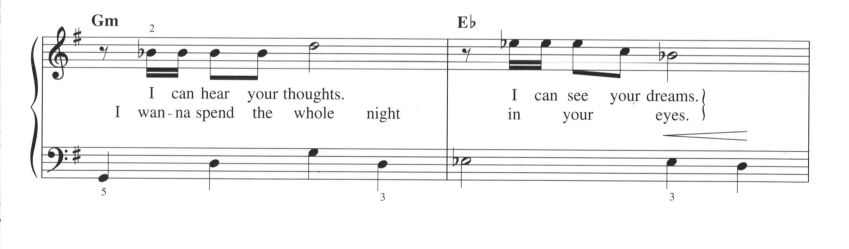

6

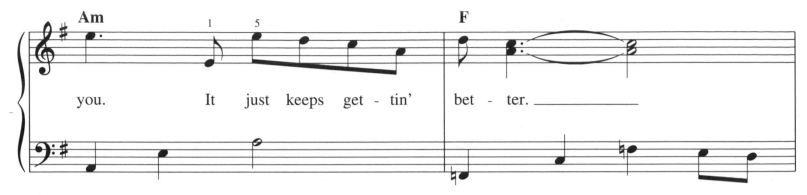

you. It just keeps get - tin' bet - ter._____

I wan-na spend the rest of my life _____ with you by my side _

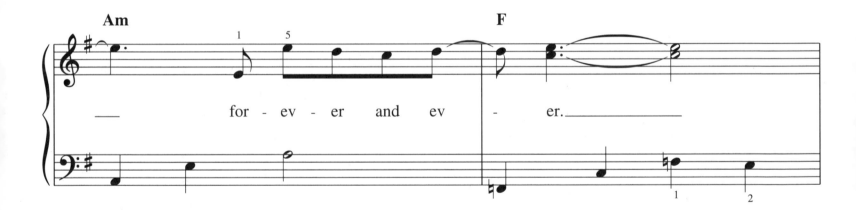

_ for - ev - er and ev - er._____

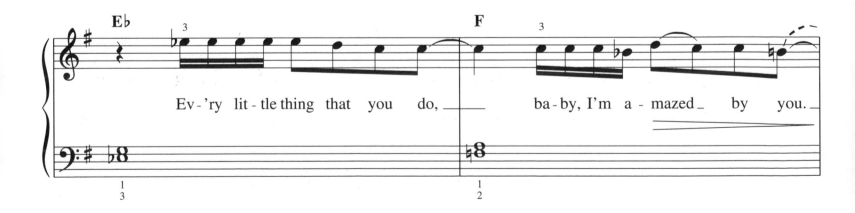

Ev - 'ry lit - tle thing that you do, ___ ba - by, I'm a - mazed _ by you._

(Instrumental)

Ev-'ry lit-tle thing that you do.___ I'm so in love with you. It just keeps get-tin'

bet - ter.___ I wan-na spend the rest of my life___

8

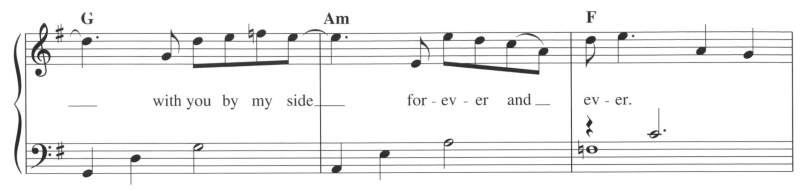

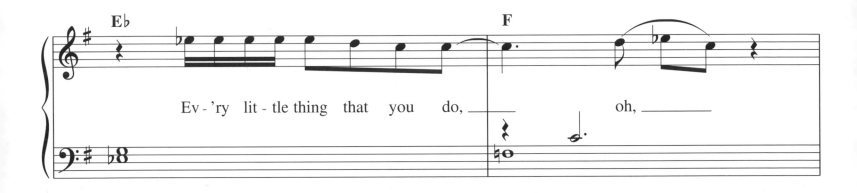

BLESSED

Words and Music by BRETT JAMES,
HILLARY LINDSEY and TROY VERGES

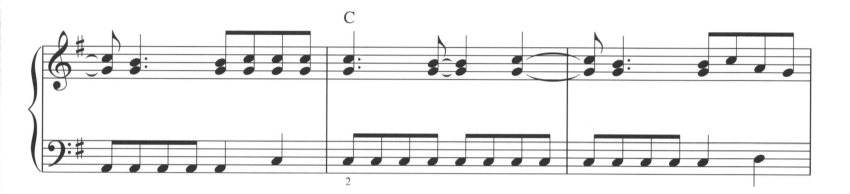

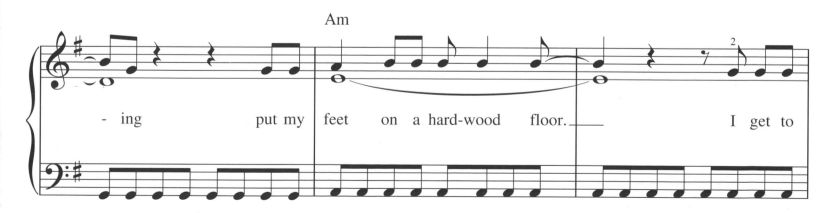

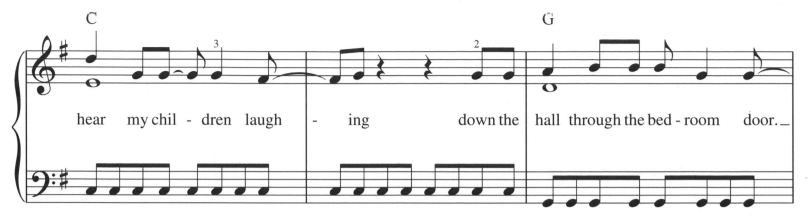

hear my chil - dren laugh - ing down the hall through the bed - room door.

— Some-times I sit on my — front porch — swing, just

soak - in' up the day. — I think to my - self I

think to my - self this world is a beau - ti - ful place. I have been

blessed._____ And I feel like I found my way._

I thank God for all__ I've been giv - en_____ at the

end of ev - er - y day._____ I have been blessed_____

__ with so much more than I__ de - serve,_____ to be

here with the ones_ who love___ me, to love them so much__ it hurts._

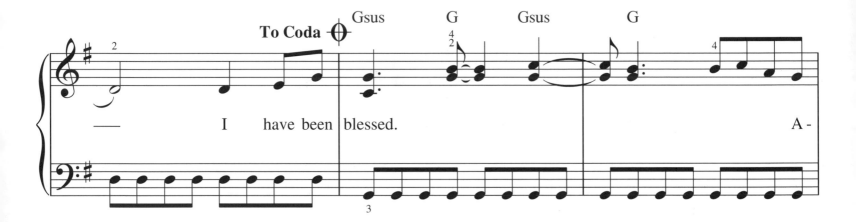

___ I have been blessed. A -

cross the crowd - ed room___ I know you know what_ I'm think -

- in' by the way I look_ at you.___ And when we're_

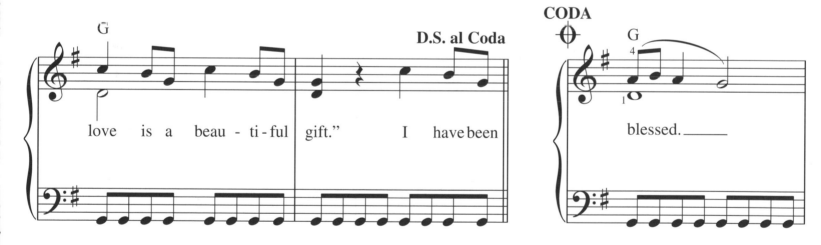

14

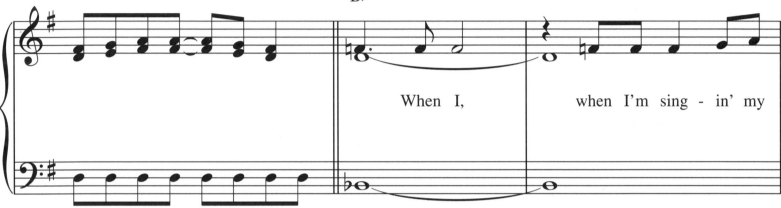

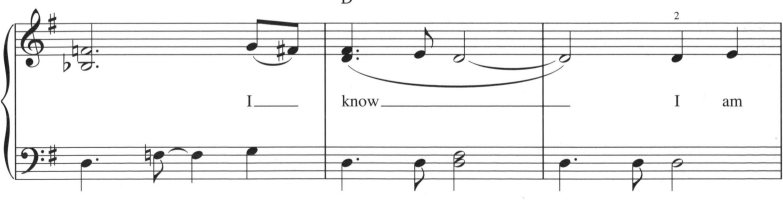

so blessed._   And I feel   like I   found_ my   way._

_____   I thank | God_ for all_ I've   been | giv - en   at the

end   of ev - er - y   day._____   I   have been | blessed_____

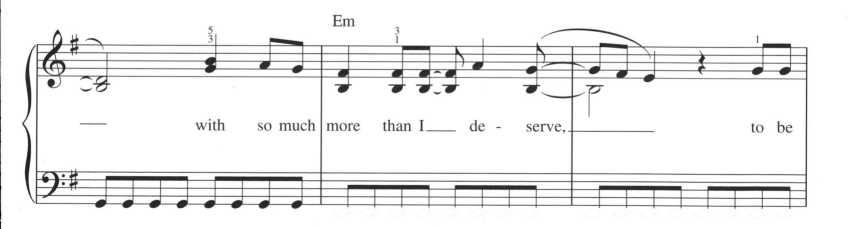

__   with   so much | more   than I__ de - serve,_____   to be

here with the ones— who love—— me, to love them so much— it hurts.—

—— I have been blessed.———— Oh,——— yes,—

— I have been blessed,———

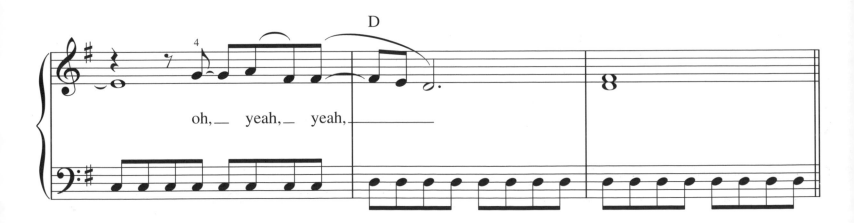

oh,— yeah,— yeah,————

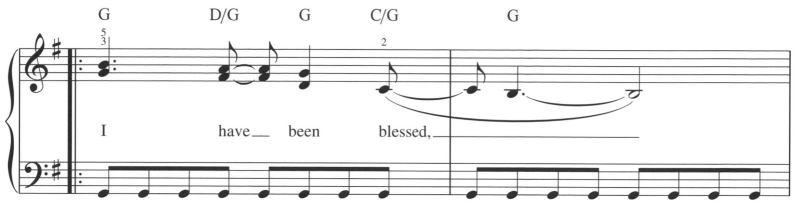

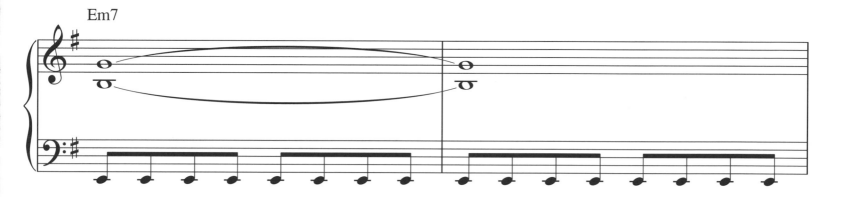

BREATHE

Words and Music by HOLLY LAMAR
and STEPHANIE BENTLEY

Moderately fast

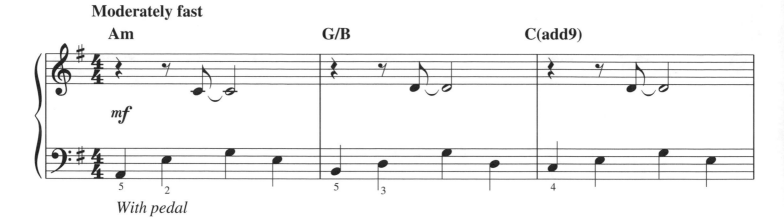

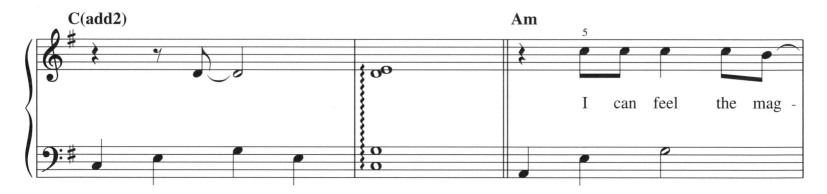

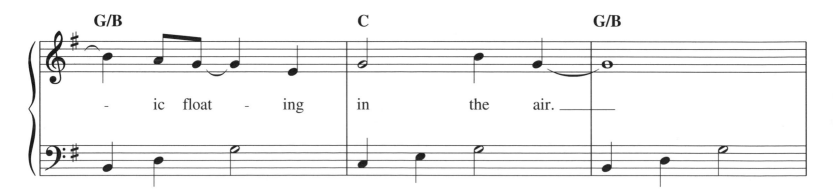

19

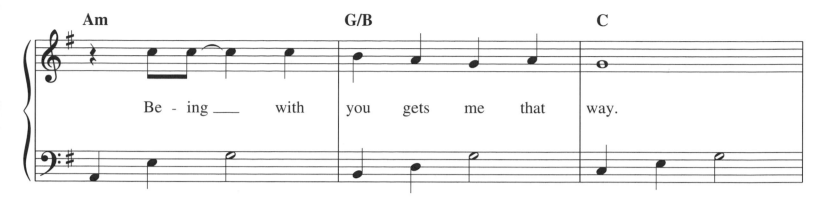

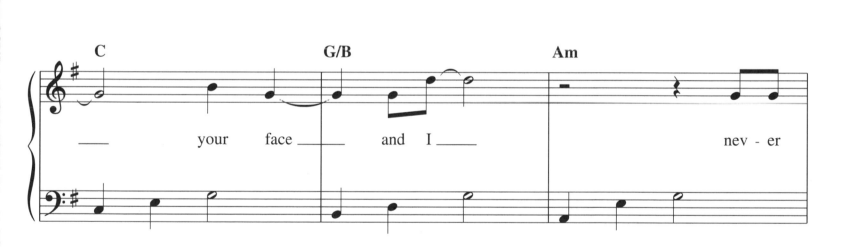

All my thoughts just seem to set - tle on the breeze _____
In a way I know my heart ___ is wak - ing up _____

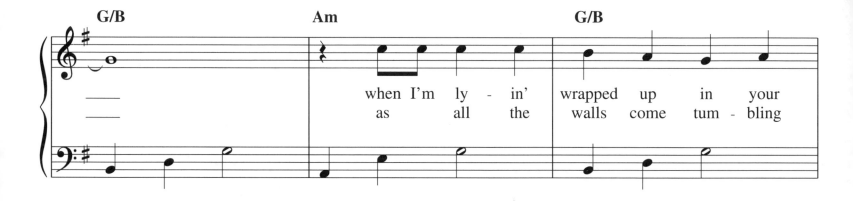

_____ when I'm ly - in' wrapped up in your
_____ as all the walls come tum - bling

arms. The whole world just
down. Clos-er than I've

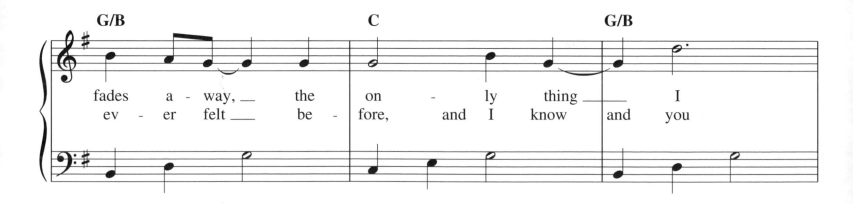

fades a - way, ___ the on - ly thing _____ I
ev - er felt ___ be - fore, and I know and you

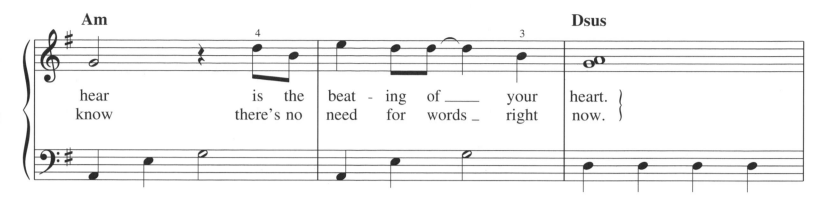

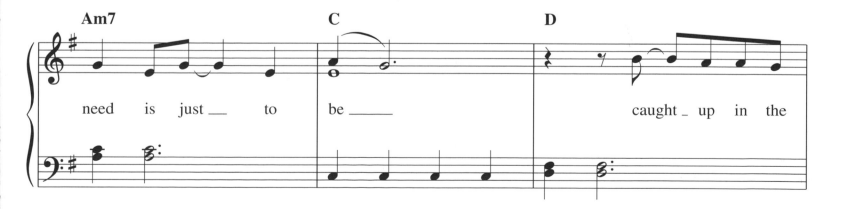

touch, the slow and stead - y rush. Ba - by, is - n't that the way___ that

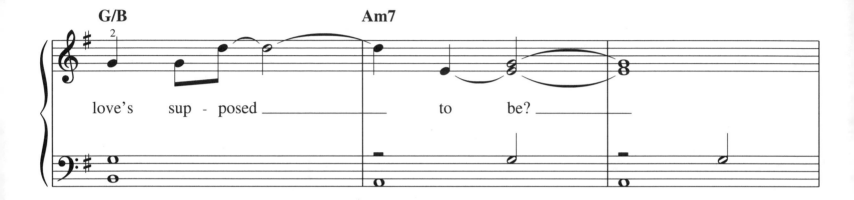

love's sup - posed ___ to be? ___

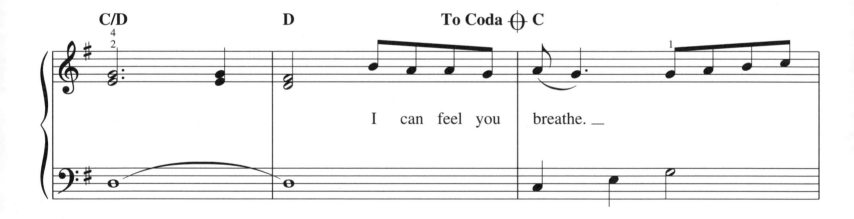

I can feel you breathe. __

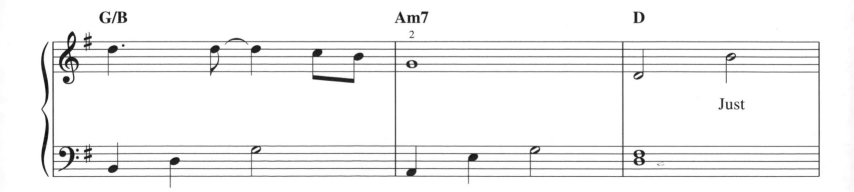

Just

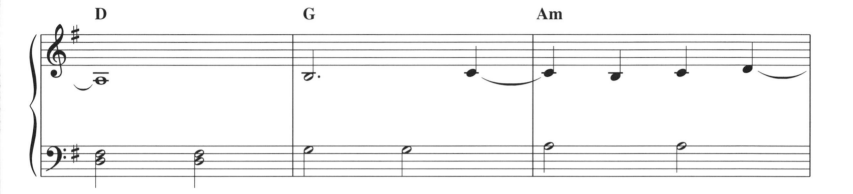

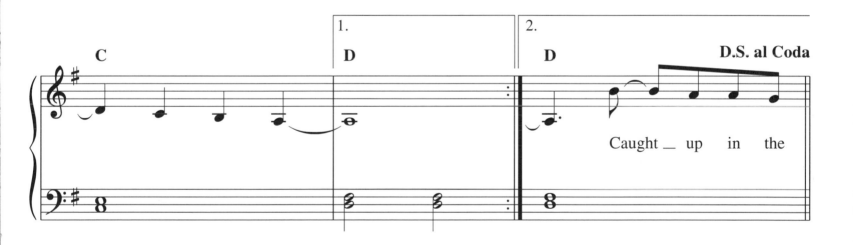

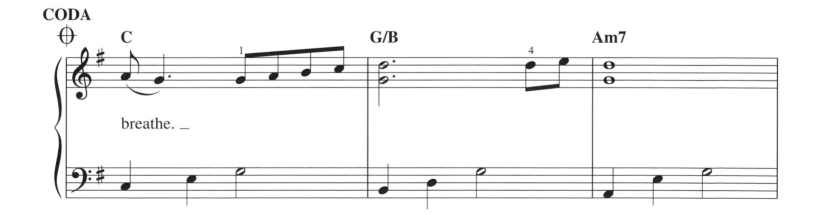

24

Just _____ breathe.

I can feel the mag -

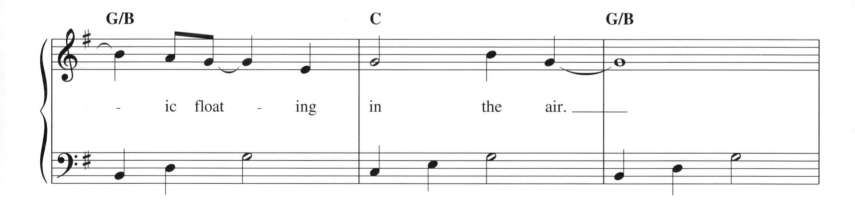

- ic float - ing in the air. _____

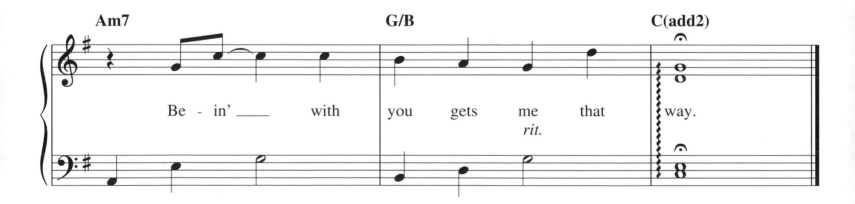

Be - in' ____ with you gets me that way.

rit.

I HOPE YOU DANCE

Words and Music by TIA SILLERS
and MARK D. SANDERS

Moderately

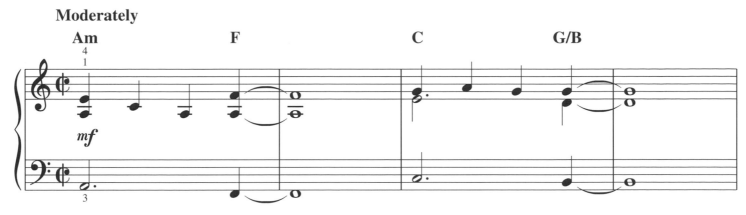

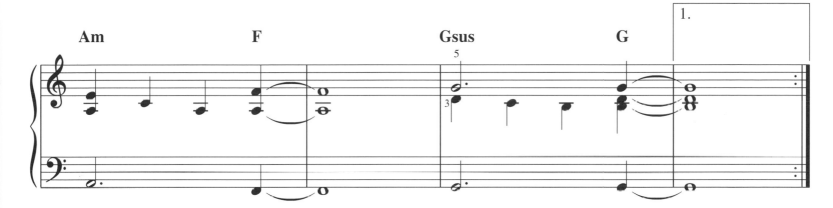

- ways   keep   that   hun - ger. _____   May you
___ of   least   re - sis - tance. _____   Liv - in'

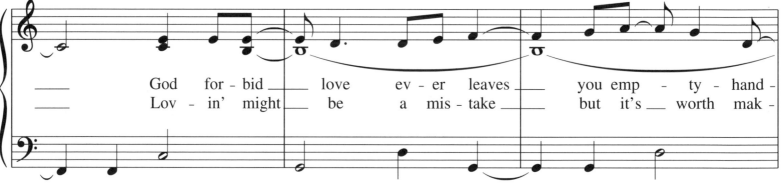

F

nev - er   take ___ one   sin - gle   breath ___ for grant - ed. _____
might mean   tak - in'   chanc - es   if they're   worth tak   - in'. _____

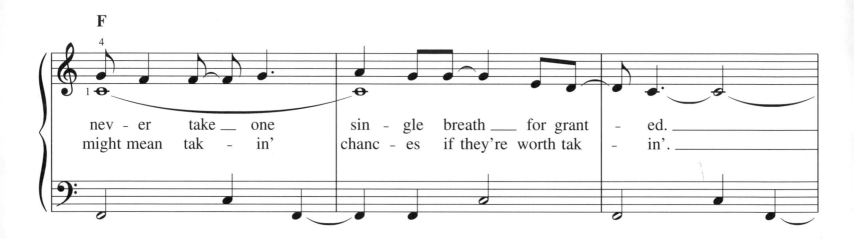

G

___   God   for - bid ___ love   ev - er   leaves ___   you emp - ty - hand -
___   Lov - in' might ___ be   a   mis - take ___   but it's ___ worth mak -

%   **F**   **G**

- ed. _____   I hope you   still ___ feel   small _ when you
- in'. _____   Don't   let ___ some   hell - bent

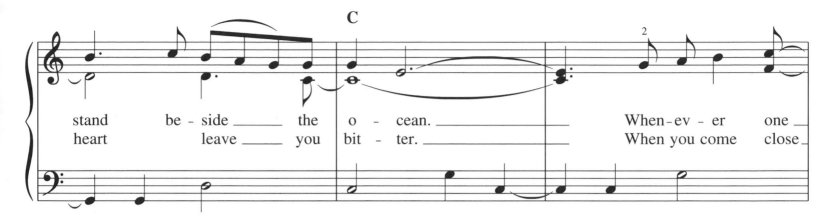

stand   be - side _____ the o - cean. _____   When-ev - er   one _
heart   leave _____ you bit - ter. _____   When you come   close_

_____ door clos - es, I _____ hope   one _ more o - pens. _____
_____ to   sell - in' out, _____   re - con - sid - er. _____

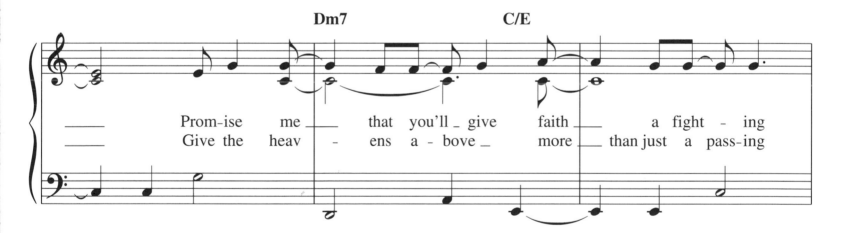

_____ Prom-ise   me _____ that you'll _ give faith _____ a fight - ing
_____ Give the heav - ens a - bove _   more _____ than just a pass-ing

To Coda ⊕

chance. _____
glance. _____   And when you get the choice to sit _ it out   or

28

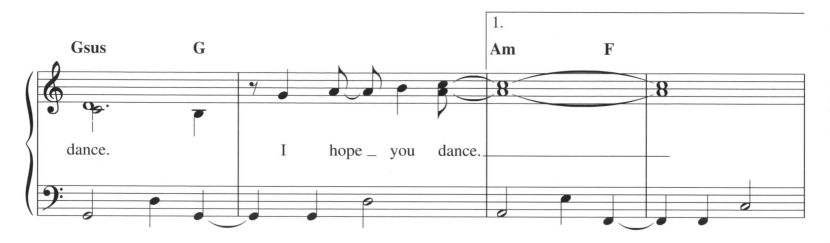

Gsus   G   1.
                           Am   F

dance.   I hope _ you dance.

C   G/B   Am   F

I hope _ you   dance.

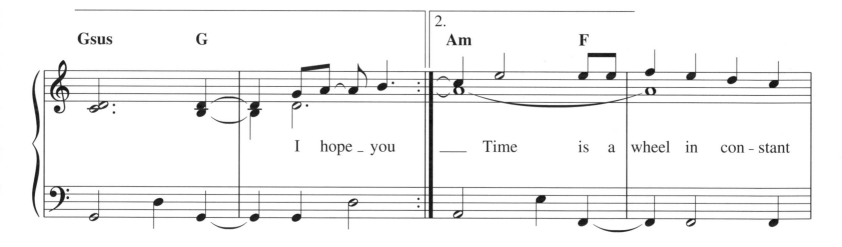

Gsus   G   2.
                          Am   F

I hope _ you   ___ Time   is a wheel in con-stant

C   G/B   Am   F

mo-tion   al - ways   roll - ing   us

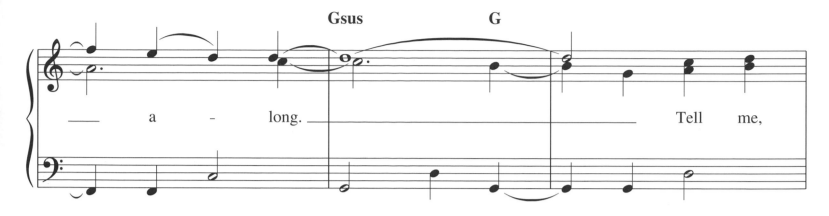

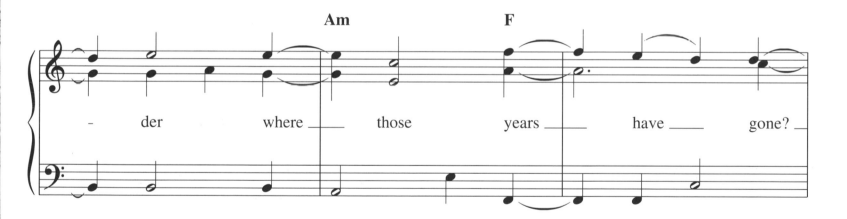

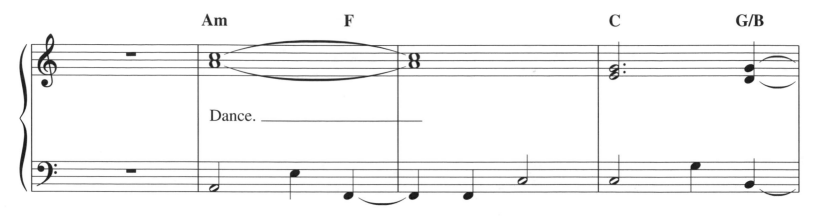

Dance. _____

I hope __ you dance. _____

I hope __ you dance. ___ Time is a

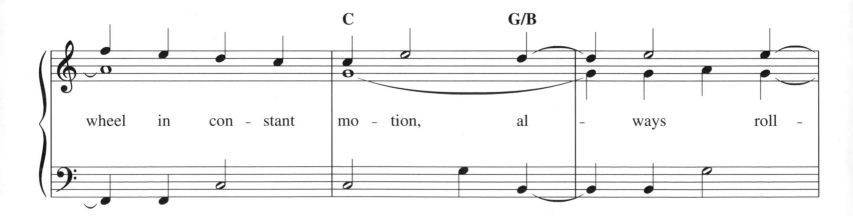

wheel in con - stant mo - tion, al - ways roll -

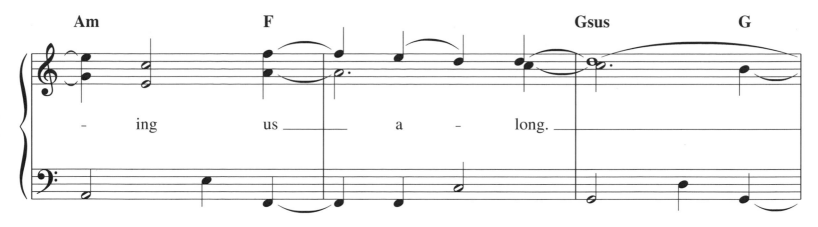

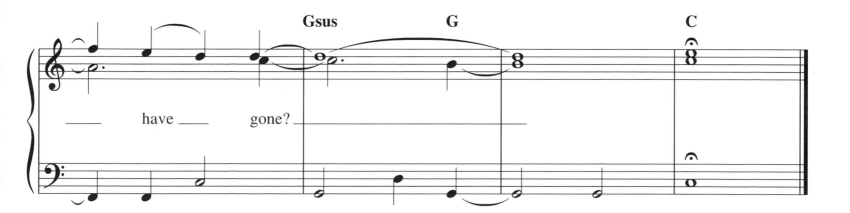

BRING ON THE RAIN

Words and Music by BILLY MONTANA
and HELEN DARLING

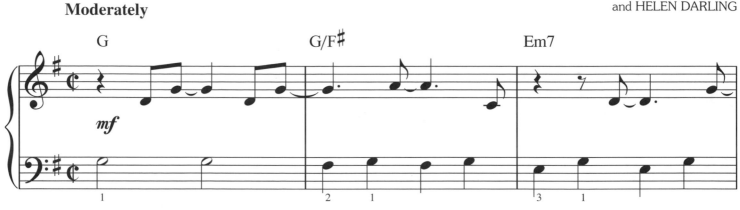

An - oth - er day has al -

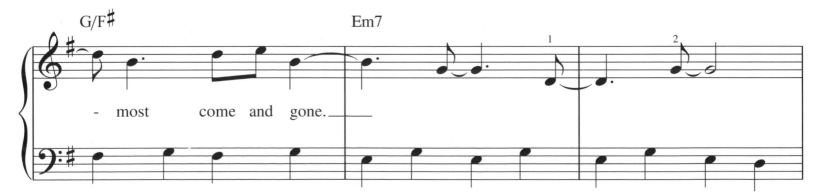

- most   come   and   gone.

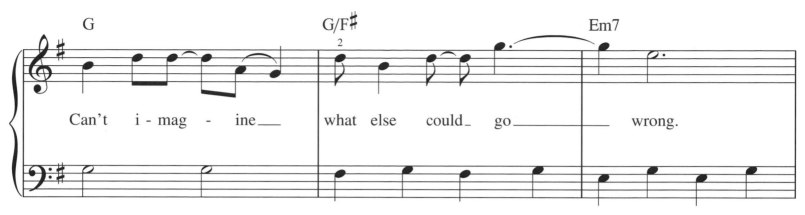

Can't i - mag - ine___ what else could_ go___ wrong.

Some - times___ I'd like___ to hide___ a - way some -

where and lock_ the door.___ A sin - gle bat - tle lost,

but not the war. 'Cause to - mor - row's an -

34

oth - er day   and I'm thirst - y   an - y - way,

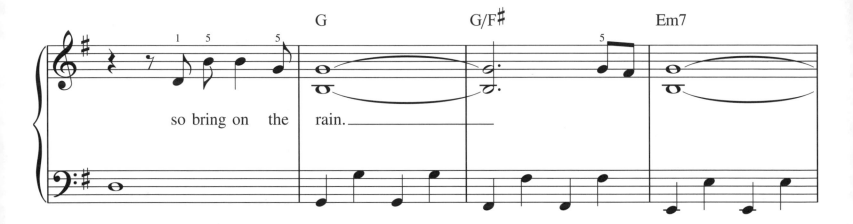

so bring on the   rain.

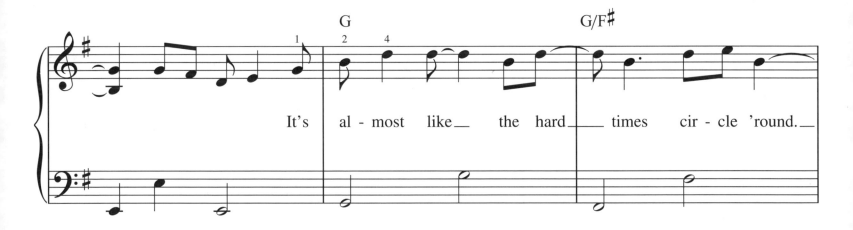

It's al - most like__ the hard__ times cir - cle 'round.__

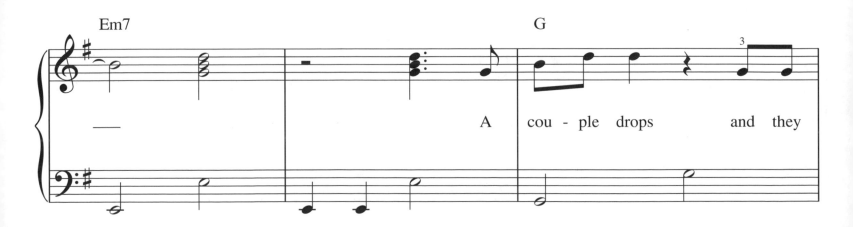

A   cou - ple drops   and they

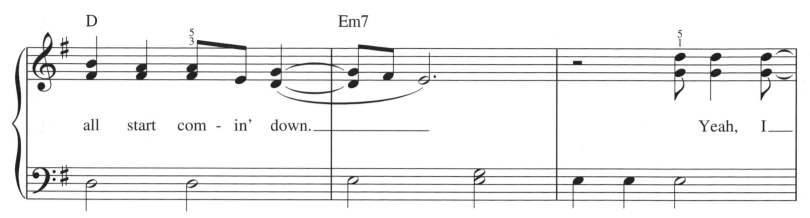

all start com - in' down._____ Yeah, I__

__ might feel__ de - feat - ed and I____ might hang__ my head..

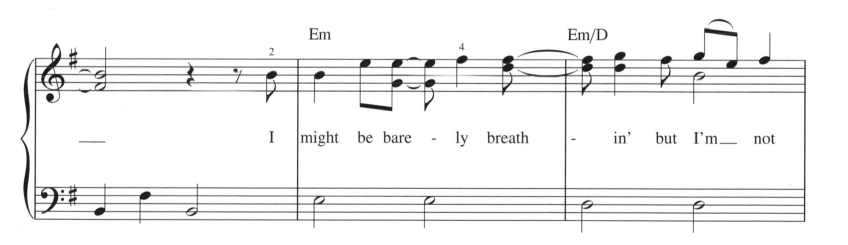

__ I might be bare - ly breath - in' but I'm__ not

dead, no. 'Cause to - mor - row's an - oth - er day

36

and I'm thirst - y   an - y - way,   so bring on the

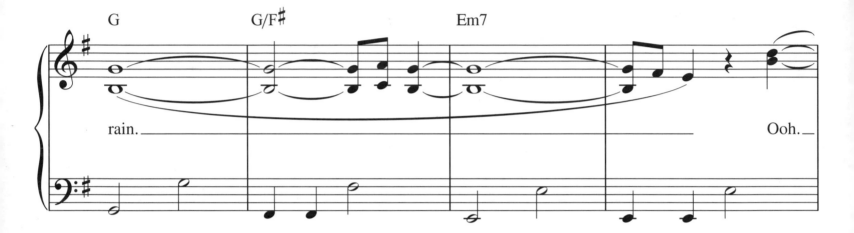

rain. _____   Ooh. __

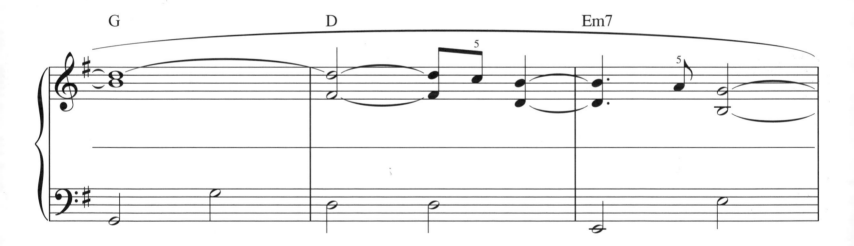

_____   No, I'm   not gon - na let it   get ___ me down,

I'm not gon-na cry._____ And I'm not gon-na lose

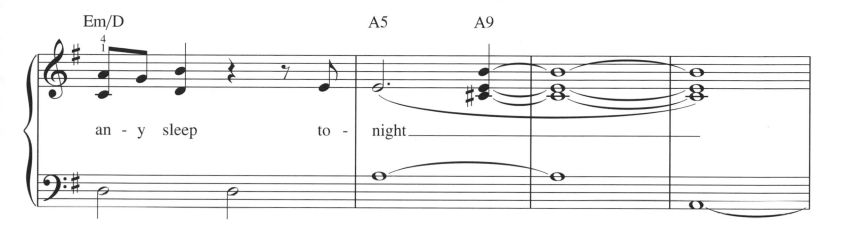

an - y sleep to - night_____

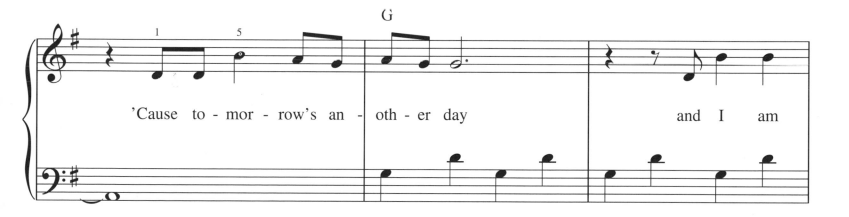

'Cause to-mor-row's an - oth-er day and I am

not a - fraid, so bring on the rain._____

Em7   C

To - mor - row's an - oth - er day

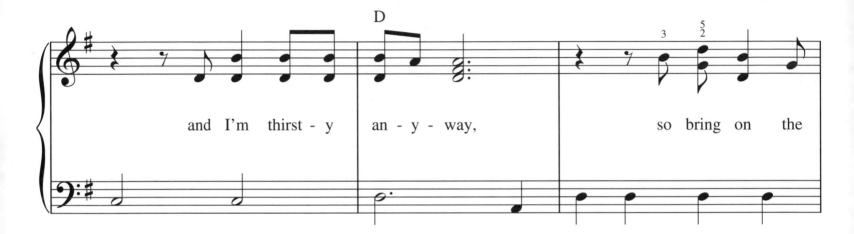

D

and I'm thirst - y   an - y - way,   so bring on the

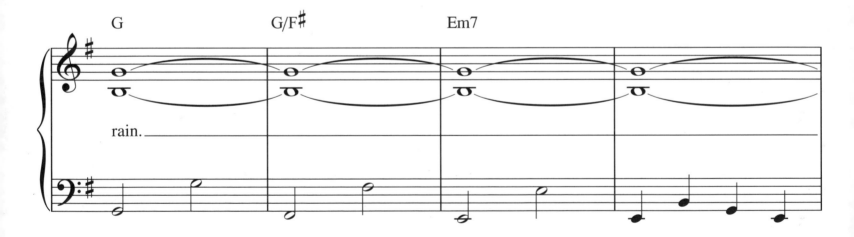

G   G/F#   Em7

rain.

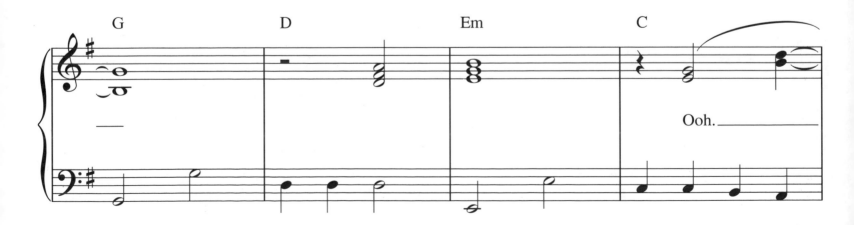

G   D   Em   C

Ooh.

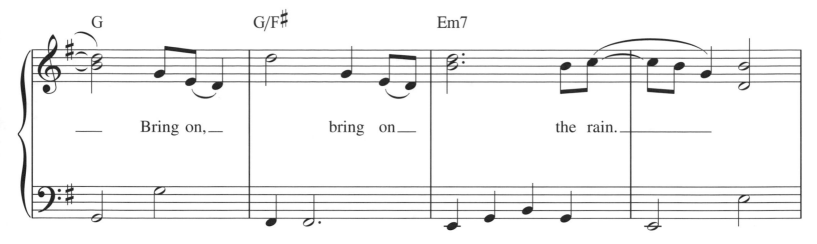

Bring on, ___ bring on ___ the rain. ___

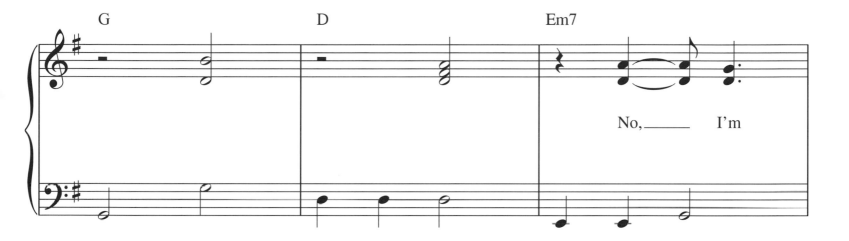

No, ___ I'm

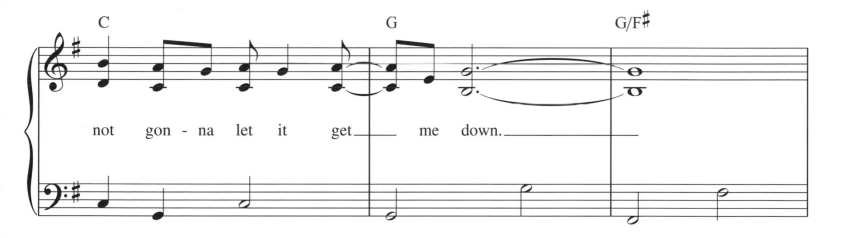

not gon - na let it get ___ me down. ___

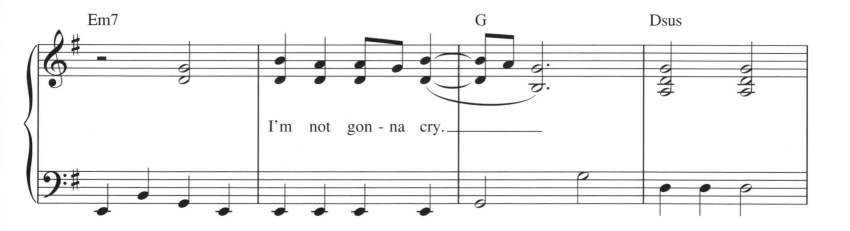

I'm not gon - na cry. ___

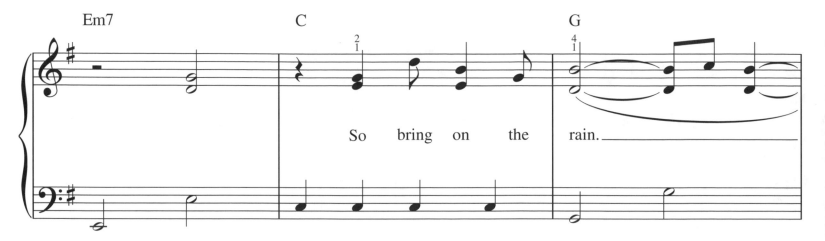

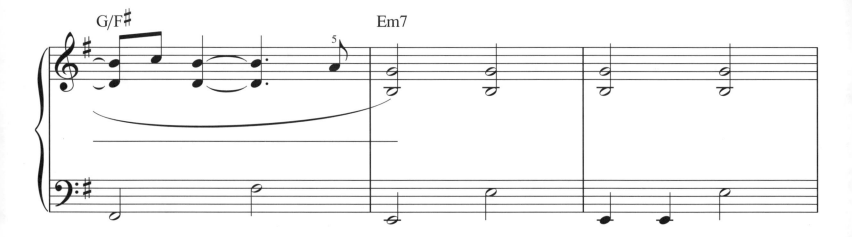

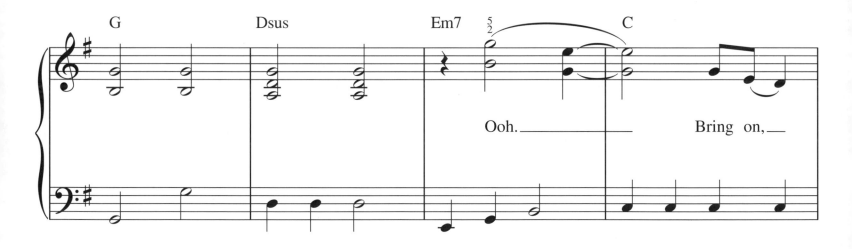

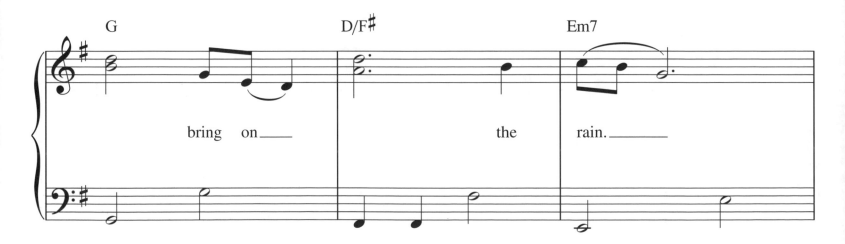

Bring on the rain.

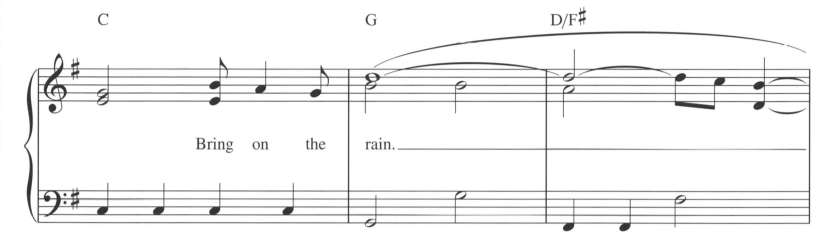

Bring on the rain.

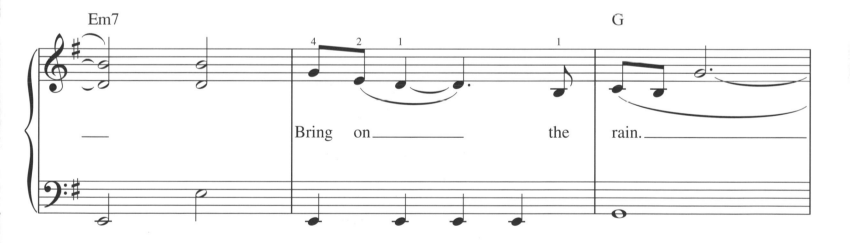

Bring on _____ the rain.

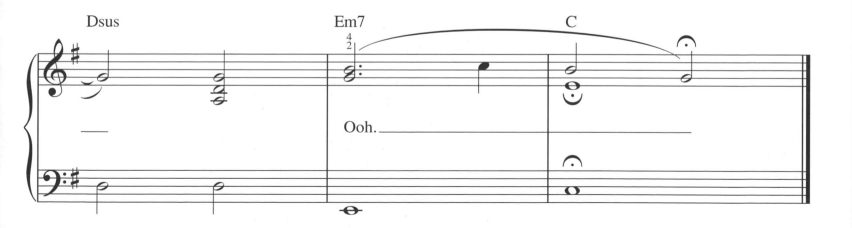

Ooh. _____

HERO

Words and Music by ENRIQUE IGLESIAS,
PAUL BARRY and MARK TAYLOR

Moderately

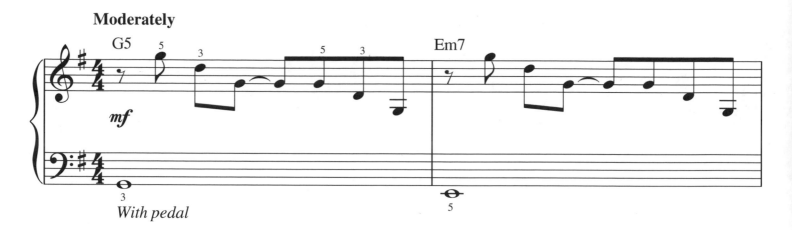

With pedal

Would you

dance   if I asked you to   dance?   Would you

run   and nev-er look   back?   Would you

44

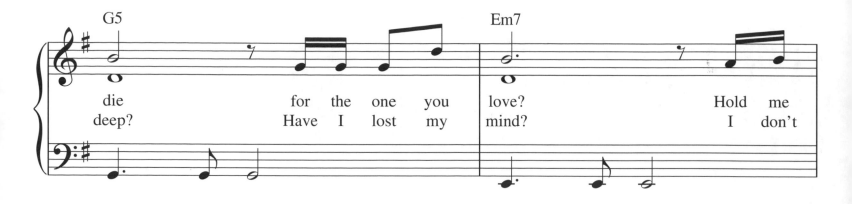

die? for the one you love?
deep? Have I lost my mind?
Hold me
I don't

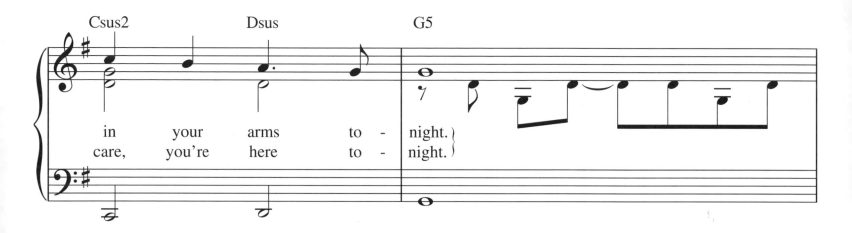

Csus2   Dsus   G5
in your arms to - night.
care, you're here to - night.

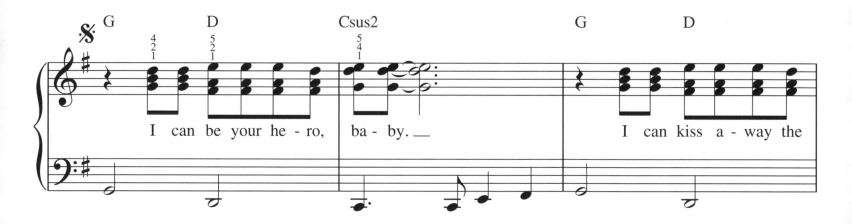

G   D   Csus2   G   D
I can be your he - ro, ba - by. ___   I can kiss a - way the

Csus2   G   D   Csus2   **To Coda** ⊕
pain.   I will stand by you for - ev - er. ___

G D C(add2)   1.

You can take my breath a-way.   Would you

2.   G5

Oh, _____

Em7   Csus2

_____ I just want to hold you.   I just want to hold you,

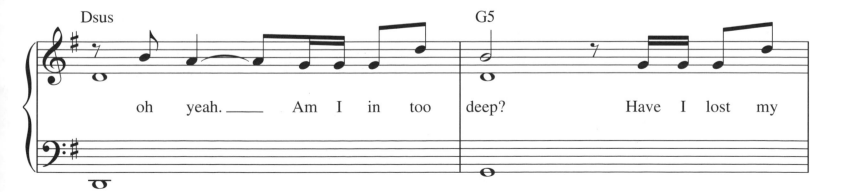

Dsus   G5

oh yeah.___ Am I in too deep?   Have I lost my

46

mind?   Well, I   don't   care   you're   here   to -

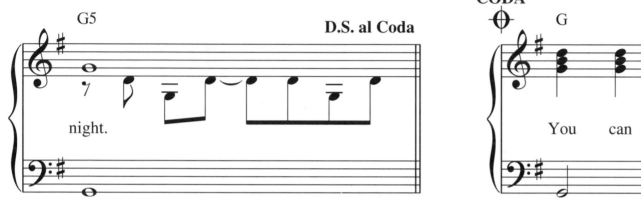

D.S. al Coda

CODA

night.

You   can   take   my

C(add2)   G   D

breath a - way. ___   I   can   be   your   he - ro,

Csus2   G   D

ba - by. ____   I   can   kiss   a - way   the

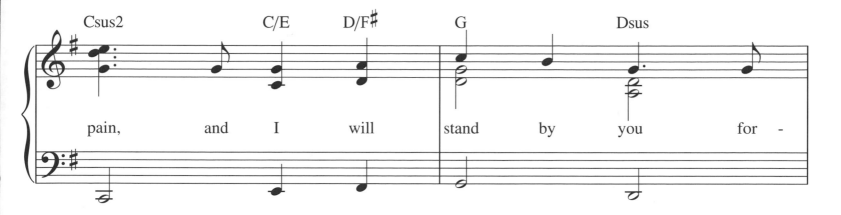

pain, and I will stand by you for -

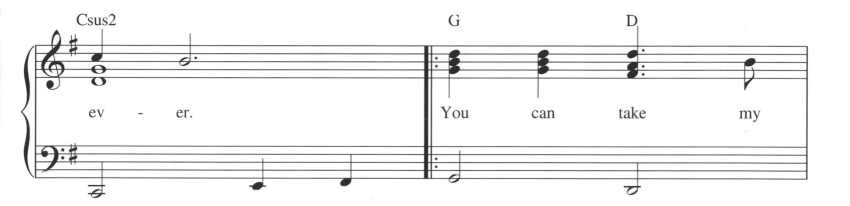

ev - er. You can take my

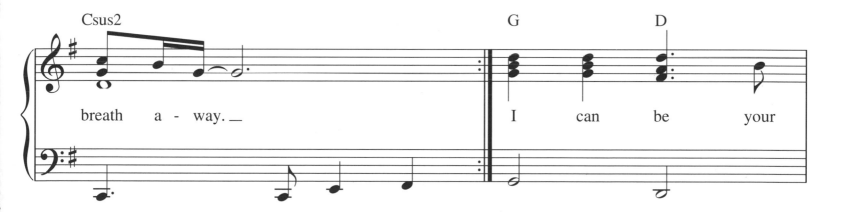

breath a - way. ___ I can be your

he - ro. _____

I NEED YOU

Words and Music by DENNIS MATKOSKY
and TY LACY

Medium Rock Ballad

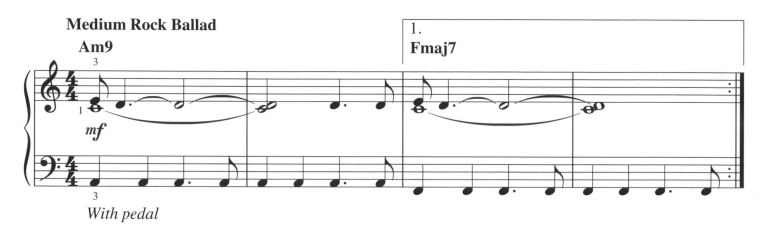

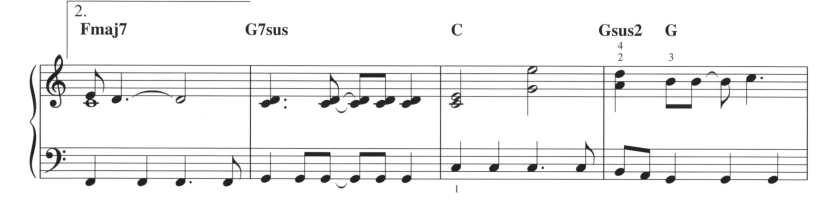

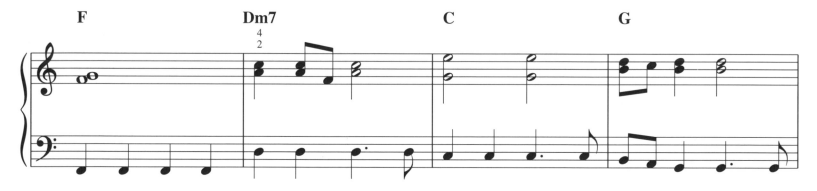

1. I don't need a lot___ of things; I can
2. *(See additional lyrics)*

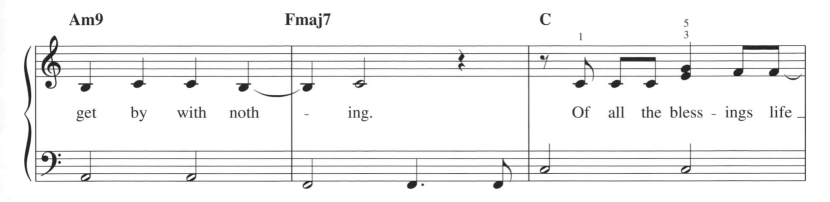

get by with noth - ing.

Of all the bless - ings life

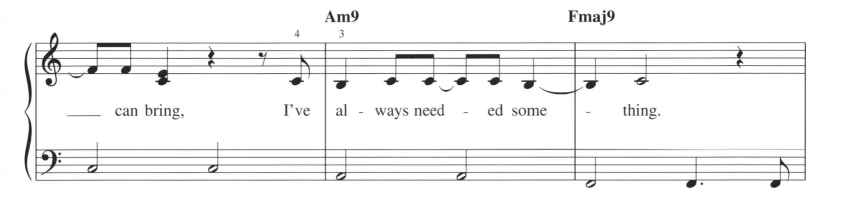

___ can bring, I've al - ways need - ed some - thing.

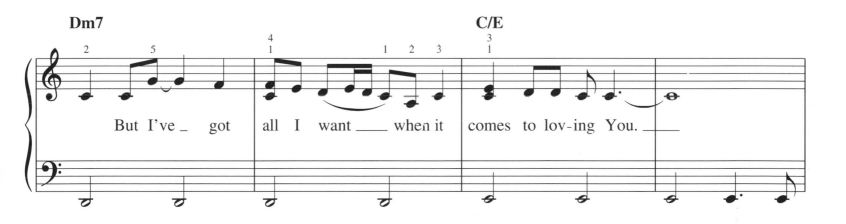

But I've _ got all I want ___ when it comes to lov-ing You. ___

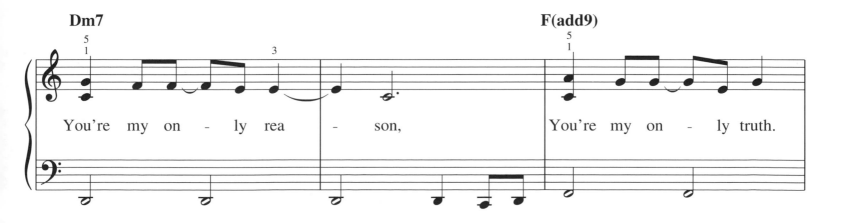

You're my on - ly rea - son, You're my on - ly truth.

Chorus

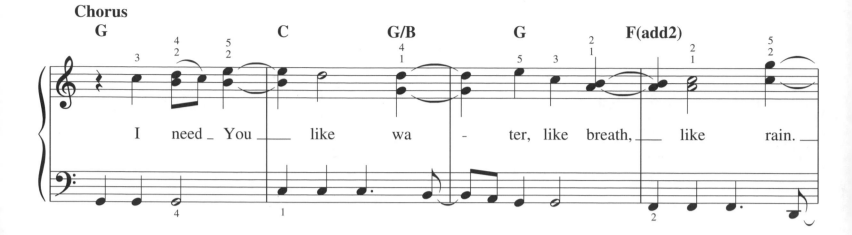

I need _ You _ like wa - ter, like breath, _ like rain.

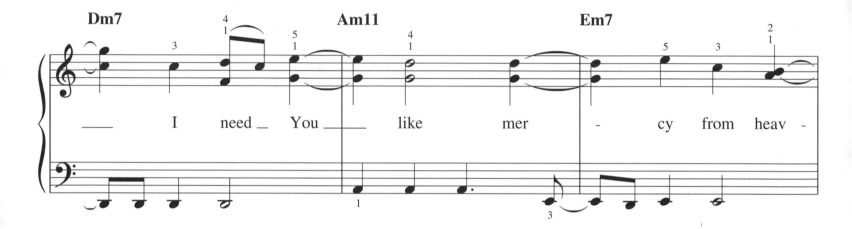

_ I need _ You _ like mer - cy from heav -

- en's gate. _ There's a free - dom in Your _

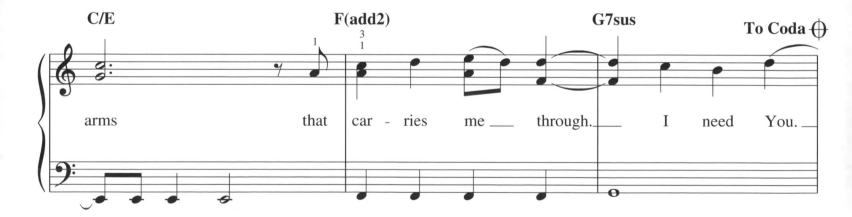

arms that car - ries me _ through. _ I need You.

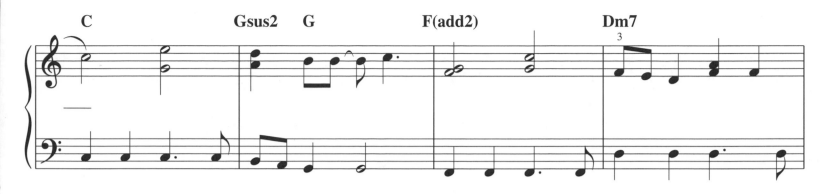

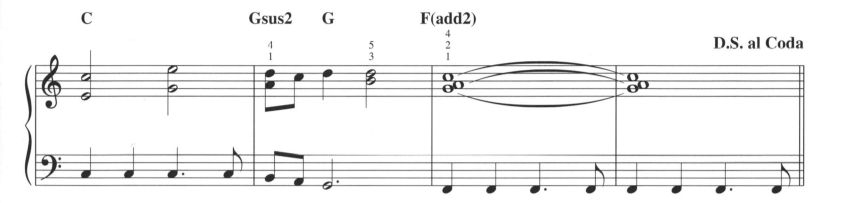

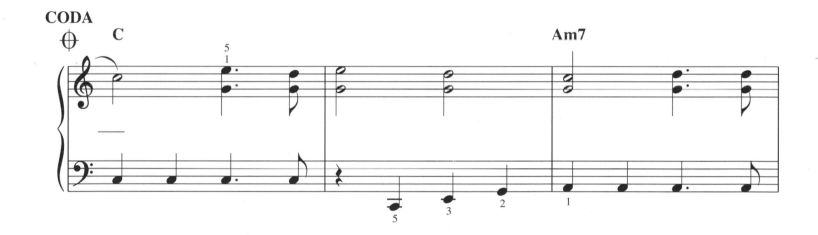

52

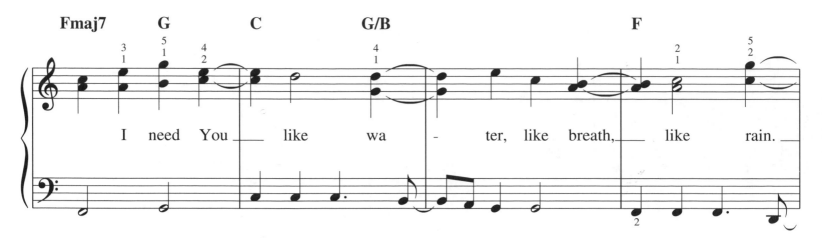

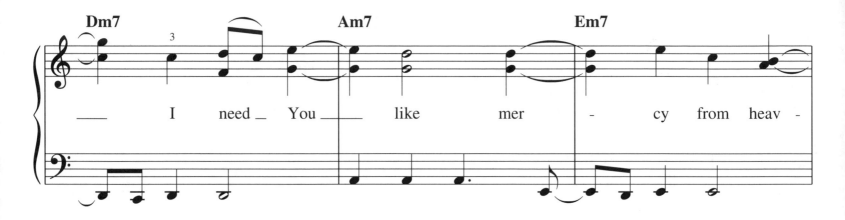

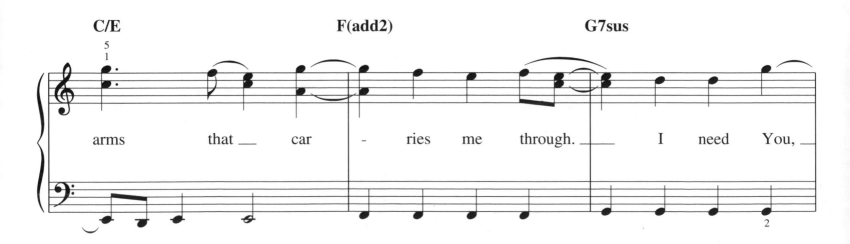

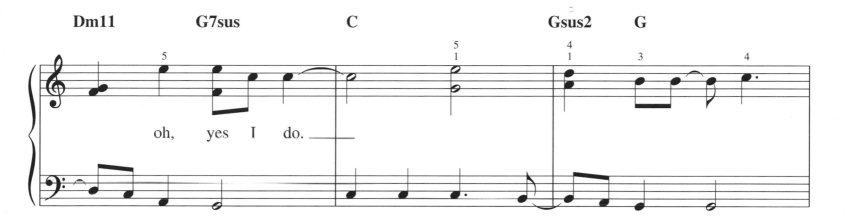

oh,   yes   I   do.

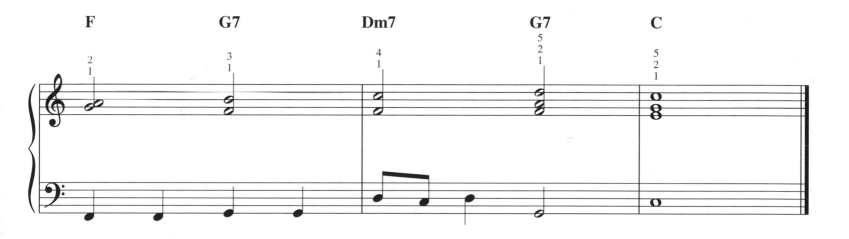

Additional Lyrics

2. You're the hope that moves me to courage again, oh yeah.
   You're the love that rescues me when the cold winds rage.
   And it's so amazing, 'cause that's just how You are.
   And I can't turn back now, 'cause You've brought me so far.
   Chorus

I'M ALREADY THERE

Words and Music by RICHIE McDONALD,
FRANK MYERS and GARY BAKER

Gently

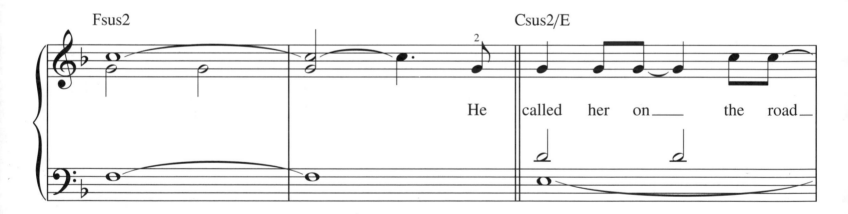

He called her on the road

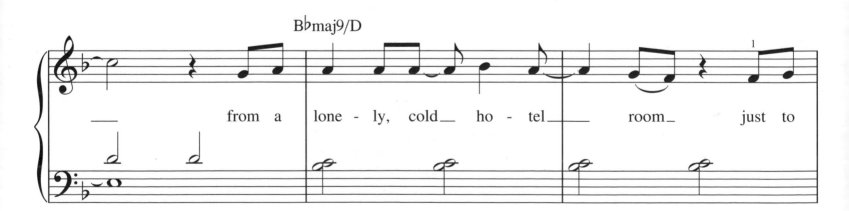

from a lone - ly, cold ho - tel room just to

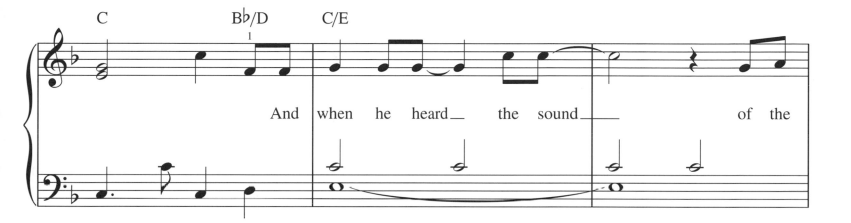

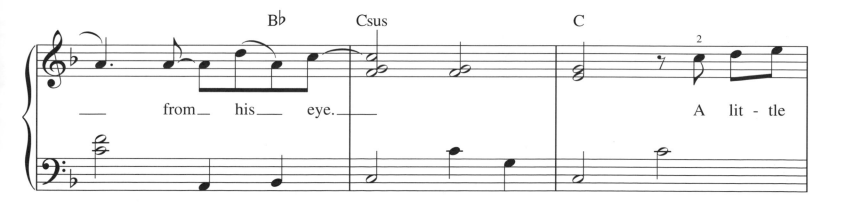

voice came on the phone and said, "Dad - dy, when you com - in' home?"

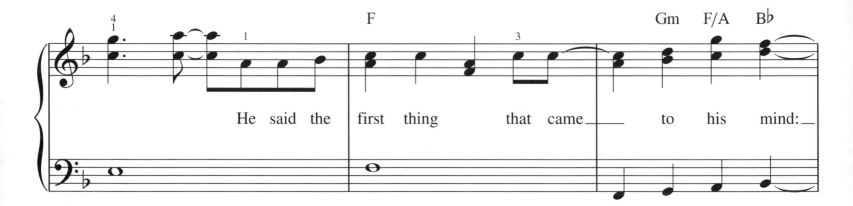

He said the first thing that came to his mind:

I'm al - read - y there. Take a look a - round.

I'm the sun - shine in your hair, I'm the

F   Bb/C   C

shad - ow on the ground.___ I'm the whis - per in the wind,___

F   C/E   Dm

___ I'm your i - mag - i - nar - y friend.___

Am7   Bb

And I know___ I'm in your prayers.___ Oh, I'm

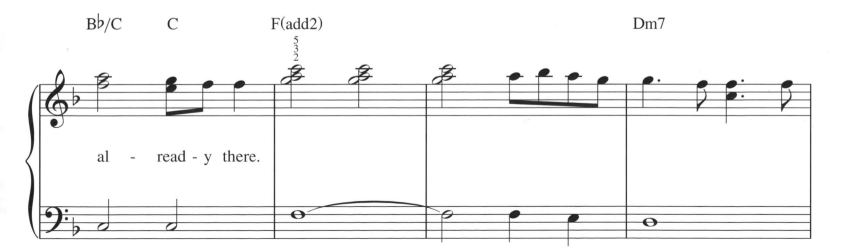

Bb/C   C   F(add2)   Dm7

al - read - y there.

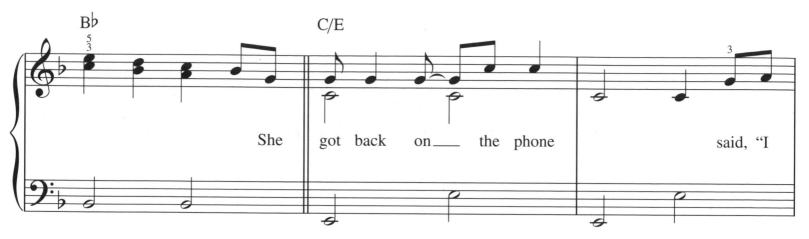

She got back on ___ the phone said, "I

real - ly miss ___ you, dar - lin'. ___ Don't wor - ry a - bout ___ the kids, ___

___ they'll be ___ al - right. ___ I wish

I was in ___ your arms, ___ ly - in' right there ___ be - side ___

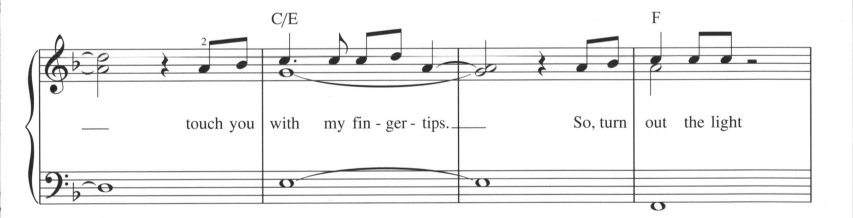

Don't make a sound___ I'm the beat of your heart,___ I'm the

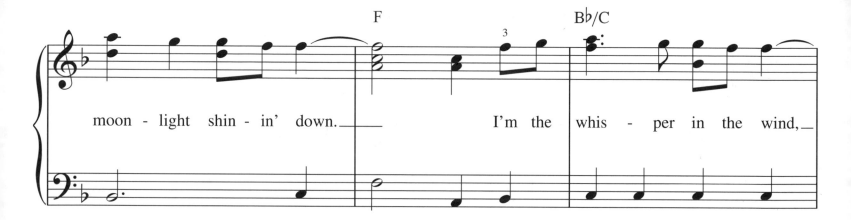

moon - light shin - in' down.___ I'm the whis - per in the wind,___

___ and I'll be there till the end.___

Can you feel___ the love that we've shared?___ Oh, I'm

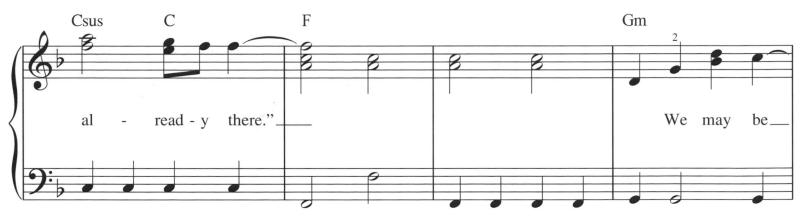

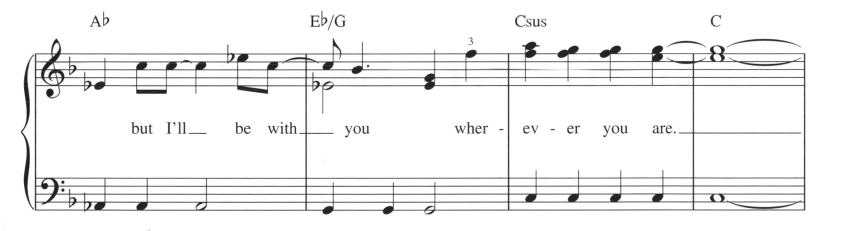

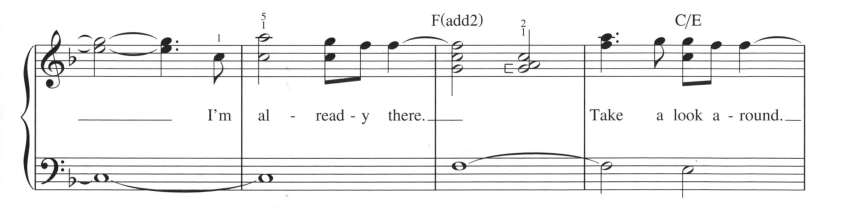

62

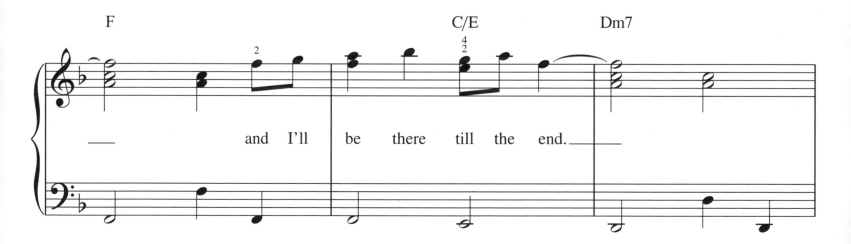

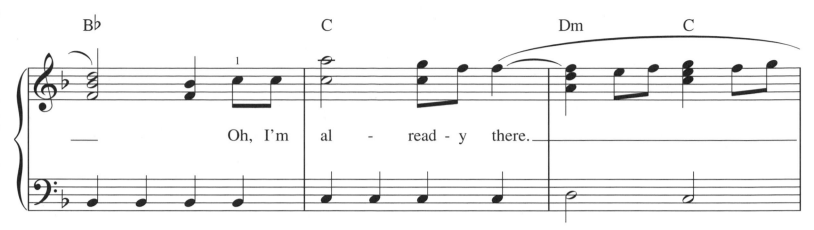

Oh, I'm al - read - y there.

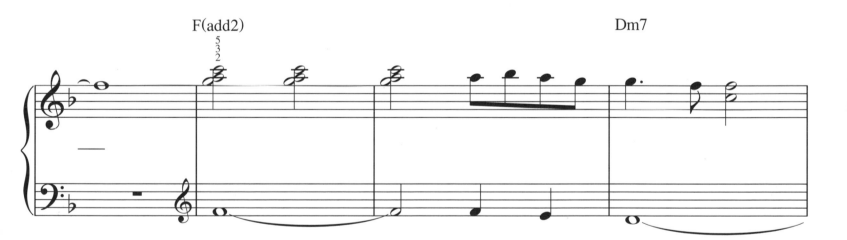

Yeah, oh, I'm al - read - y there.

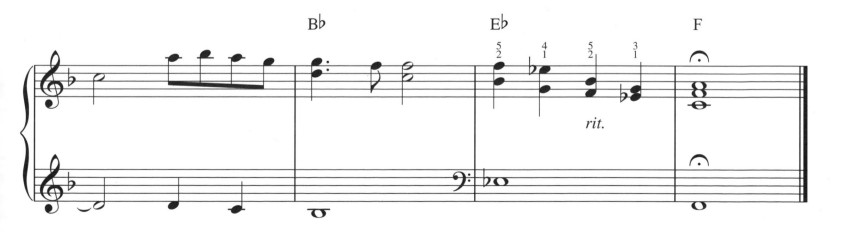

IT'S YOUR LOVE

Words and Music by
STEPHONY E. SMITH

Moderately

Male: Danc-in' in the dark, _____ mid-dle of the night. _____

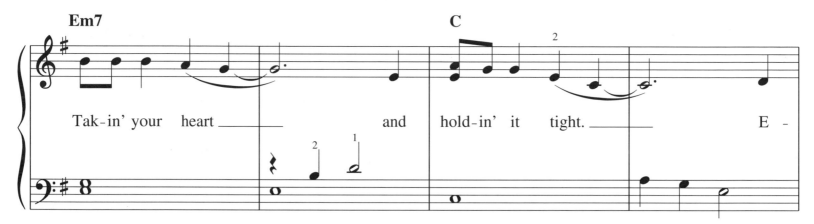

Tak-in' your heart _____ and hold-in' it tight. _____ E-

mo-tion-al touch _____ touch-in' my skin, _____ and

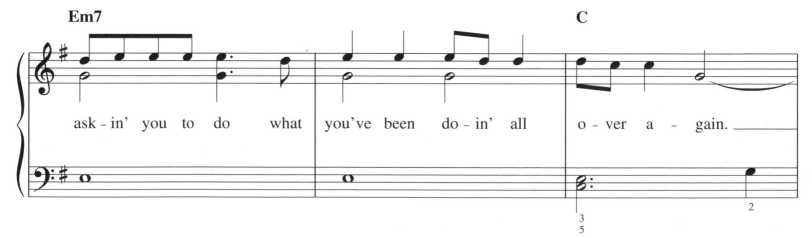

ask-in' you to do what you've been do-in' all o-ver a-gain. _____

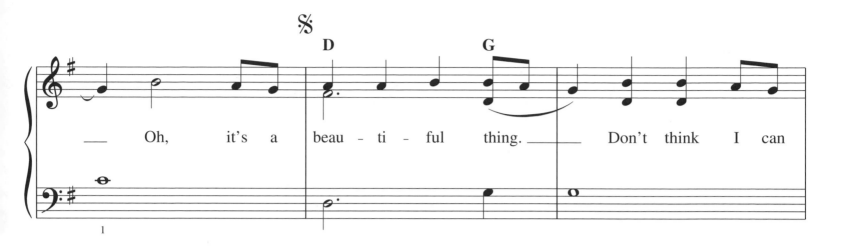

Oh, it's a beau - ti - ful thing. ___ Don't think I can

keep it all in. ___ I just got - ta let you know ___

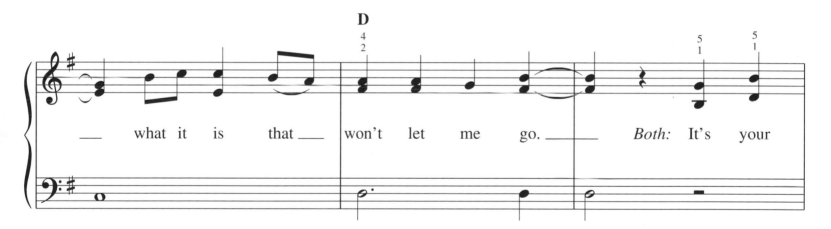

___ what it is that ___ won't let me go. ___ *Both:* It's your

love. _____ It just does some - thin' to me.

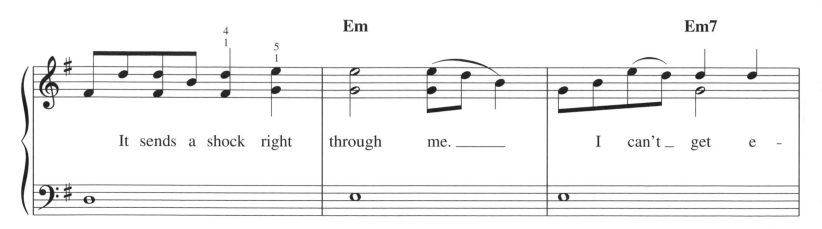

It sends a shock right through me._____ I can't_ get e-

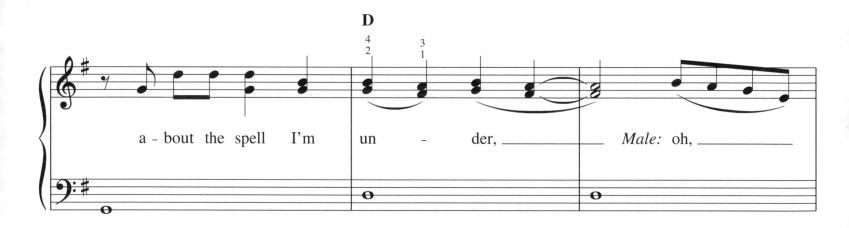

nough._____ And if you won - der_____

a - bout the spell I'm un - der,_____ *Male:* oh,_____

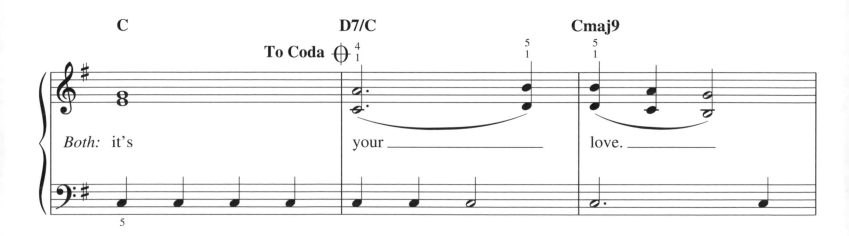

Both: it's your _____ love._____

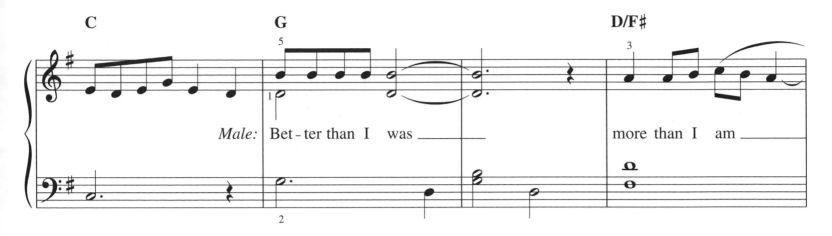

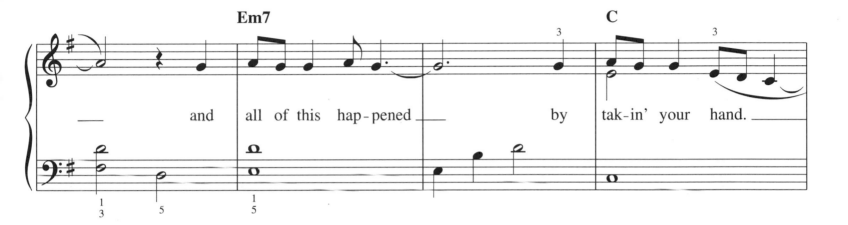

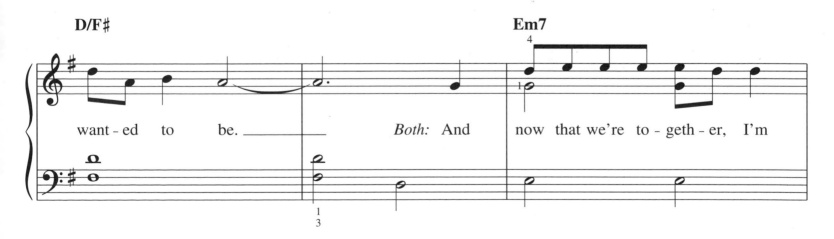

68

strong-er than ev-er. I'm hap-py and free. Oh, it's a

your _____ love. Whoa. _____ It's

your _____ love. _____ It's
mp
rit.

your _____ love. _____

MY LIST

Words and Music by RAND BISHOP
and TIM JAMES

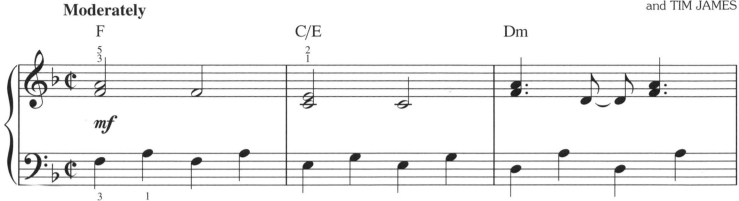

Un - der an old___ brass   pa - per - weight___
Would-n't change the   course of fate___

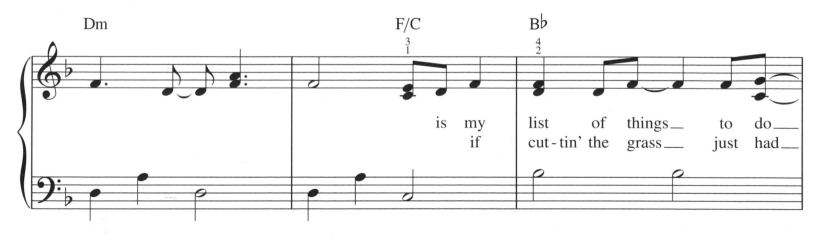

is my   list   of things___   to do___
if   cut - tin' the grass___   just had___

to - day.
to wait.

'Cause

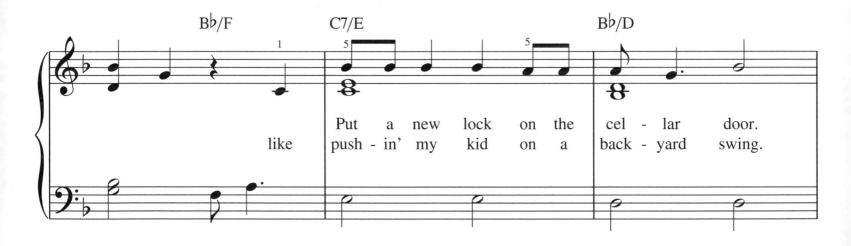

Go to the bank___ and the hard - ware store.
I've got more im - por - tant things

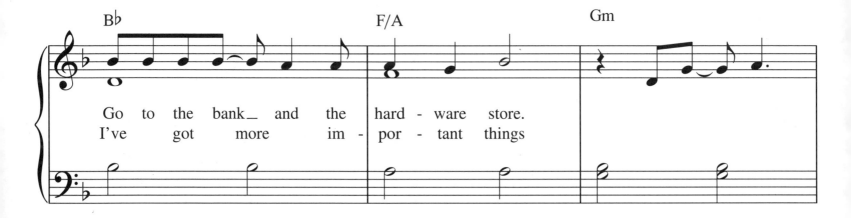

like

Put a new lock on the cel - lar door.
push - in' my kid on a back - yard swing.

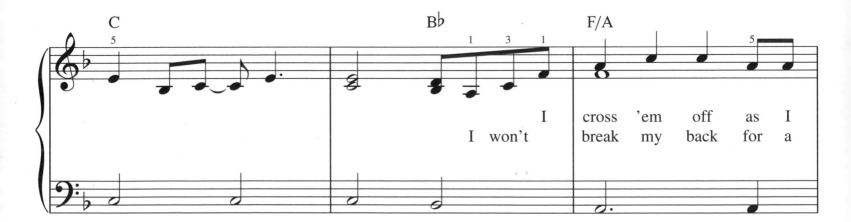

I
I won't

cross 'em off as I
break my back for a

get 'em done. But when this sun is set there's
mil - lion bucks I can't take to my grave, so why

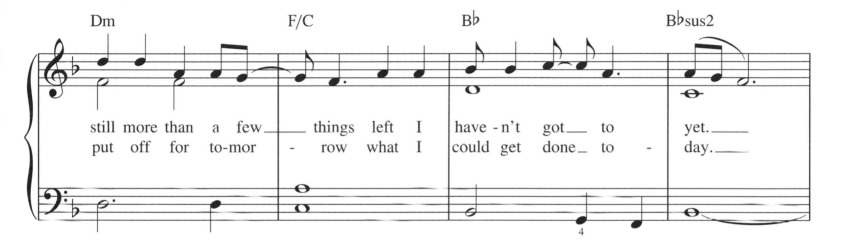

still more than a few____ things left I have -n't got__ to yet.____
put off for to-mor - row what I could get done__ to - day.____

Like Go } for a walk, say a lit - tle prayer,
go

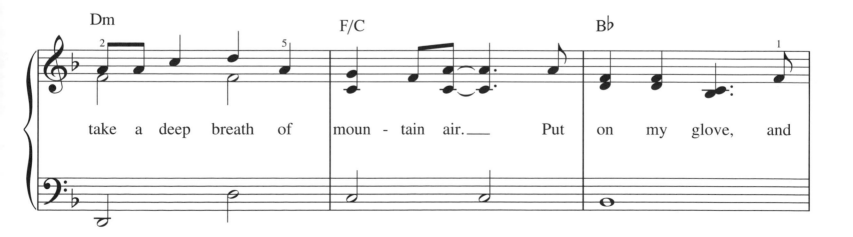

take a deep breath of moun - tain air.___ Put on my glove, and

72

play some catch.__ It's time that I make time__ for that.

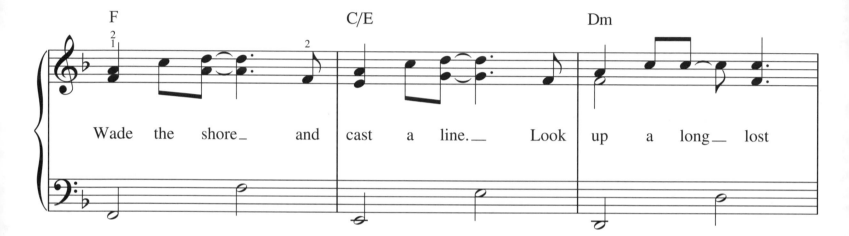

Wade the shore__ and cast a line.__ Look up a long__ lost

friend of mine.__ Sit on the porch__ and give my girl

a kiss.__ Start liv - in', that's the next__ thing on my

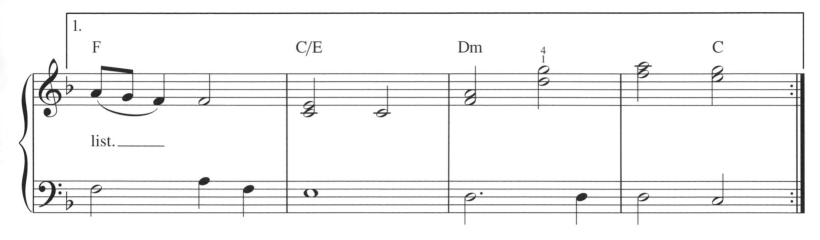

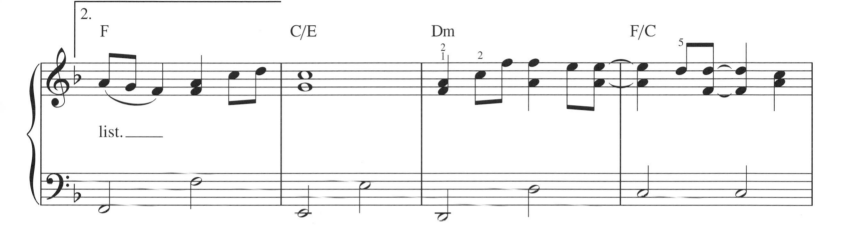

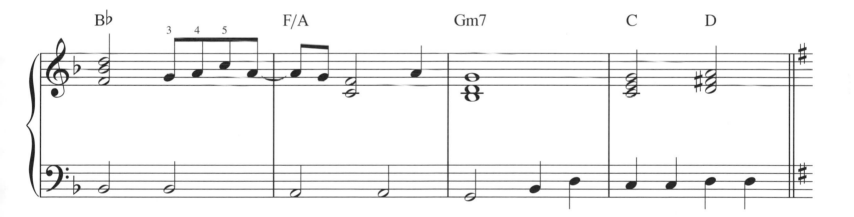

Raise a lit - tle hell, laugh till it hurts, put an ex - tra five in the

74

plate at church. Call up my folks just to chat.___ It's

time that I make time___ for that. Stay up late___ and

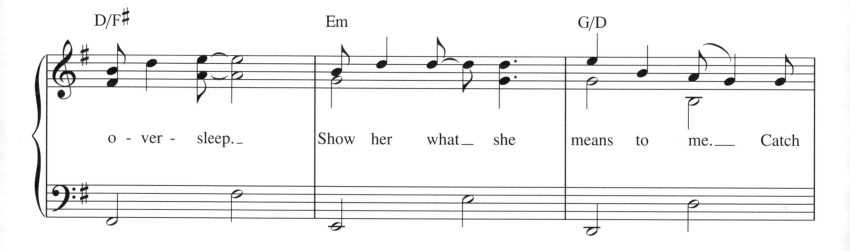

o - ver - sleep.___ Show her what___ she means to me.___ Catch

up on all the things___ I've al - ways missed._____ Just start

liv - in' that's the next thing on my list.

Un - der an old brass

pa - per - weight is my list of things to do

to - day.

ME AND YOU

Words and Music by SKIP EWING
and RAY HERNDON

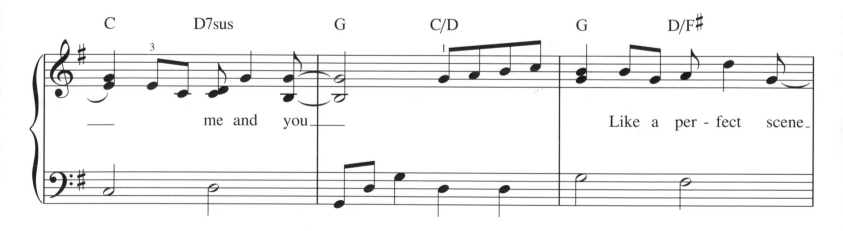

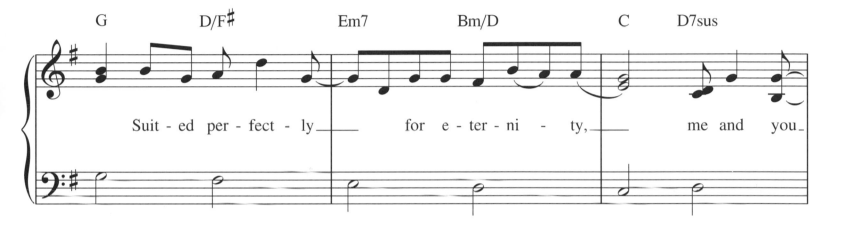

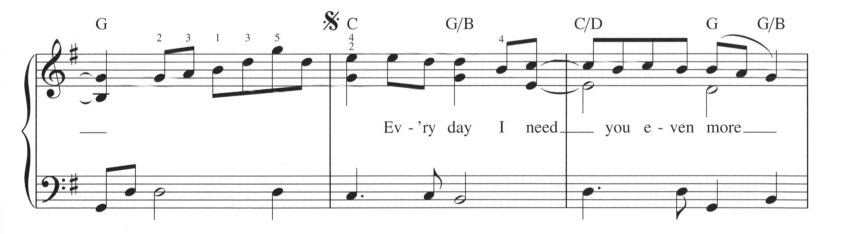

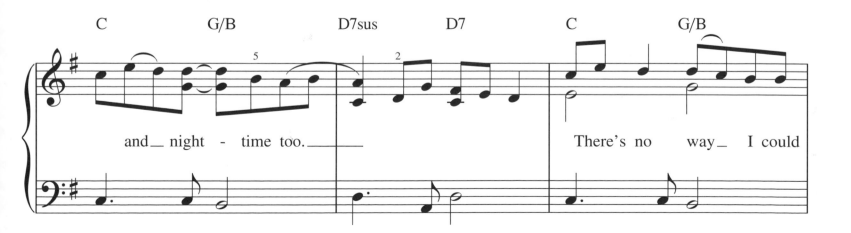

78

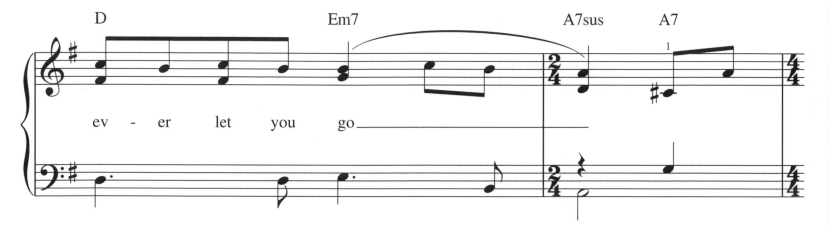

ev - er let you go_____

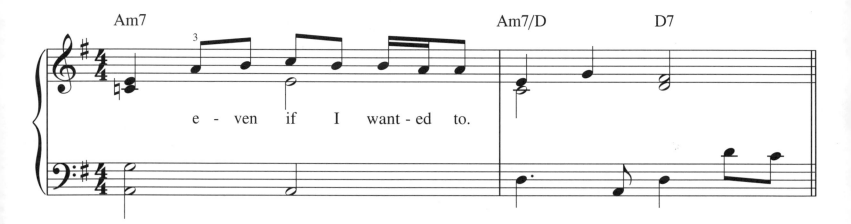

e - ven if I want-ed to.

Ev - 'ry day I live,____ try my best to give____
Instrumental solo
Or - di - nar - y? No,____ real - ly don't think so.____

____ all I have to you.____
____ Just a pre - cious few____

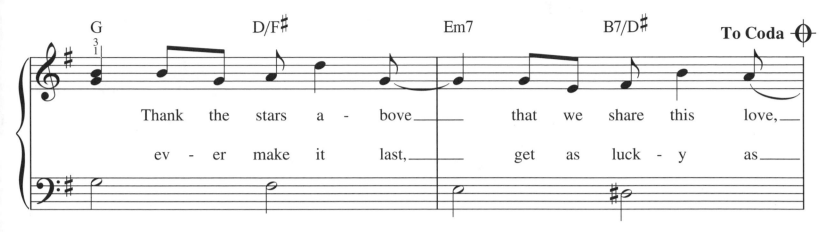

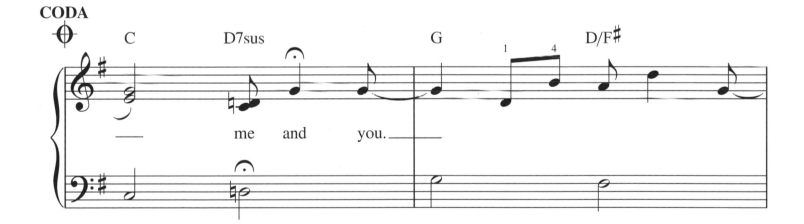

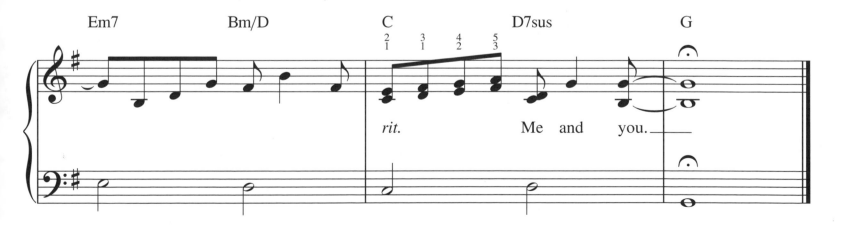

ONE MORE DAY
(With You)

Words and Music by STEVEN DALE JONES
and BOBBY TOMERLIN

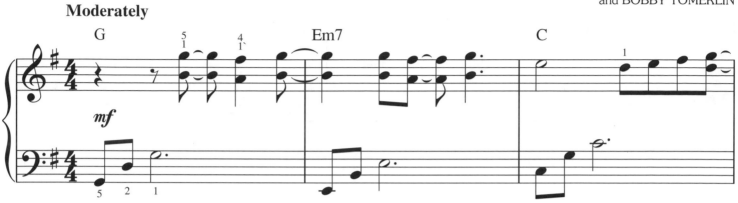

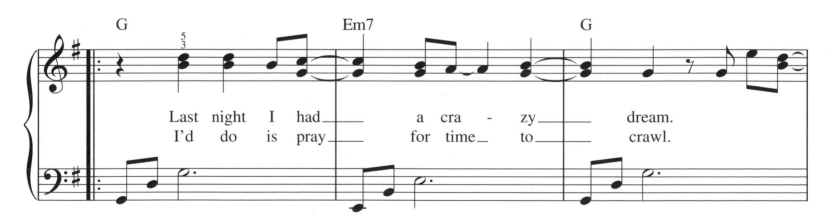

Last night I had a cra - zy dream.
I'd do is pray for time to crawl.

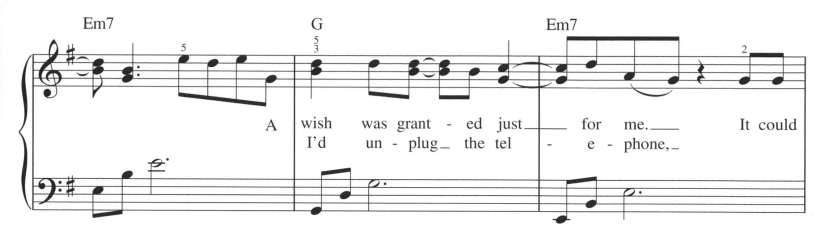

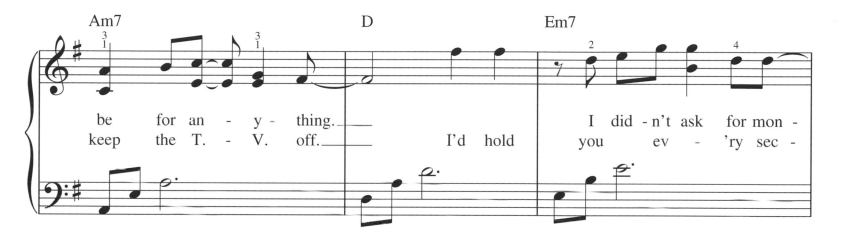

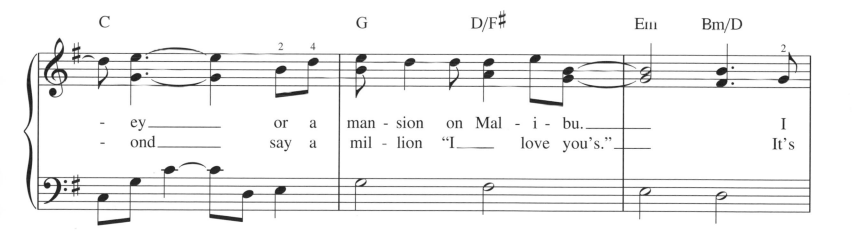

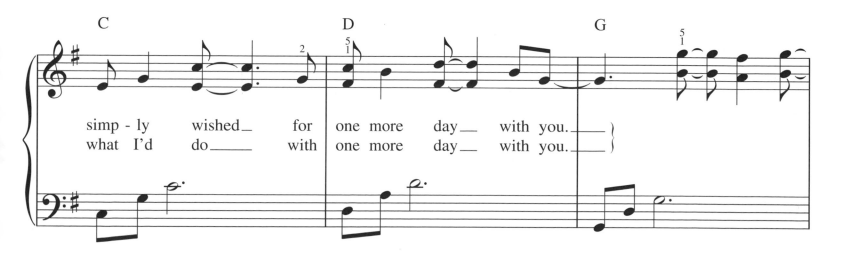

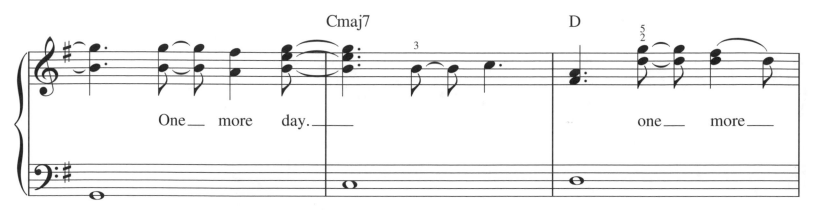

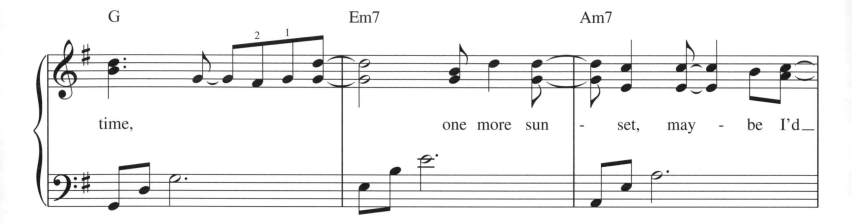

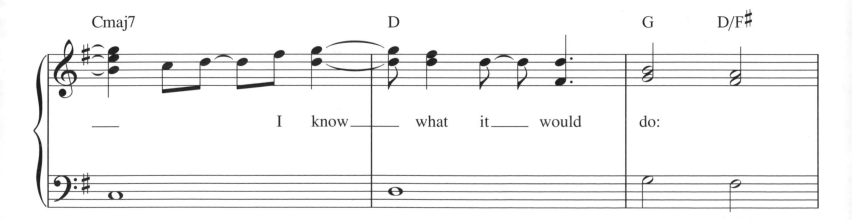

leave me wish - in' still___ for one more day___ with you.___

One___ more day.___

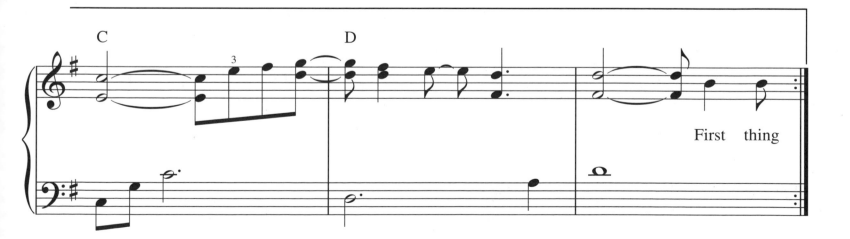

First thing

84

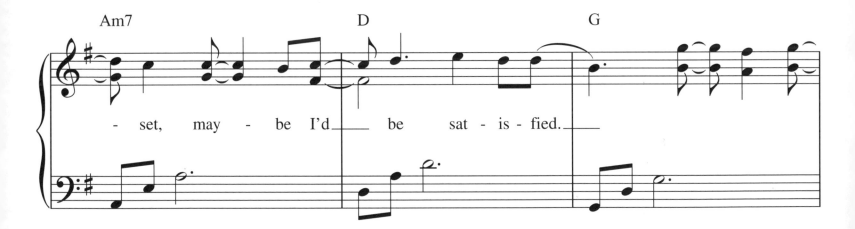

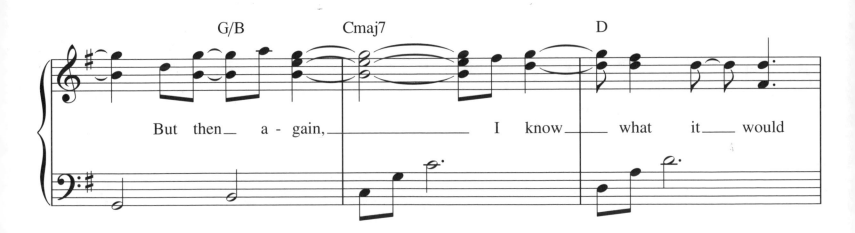

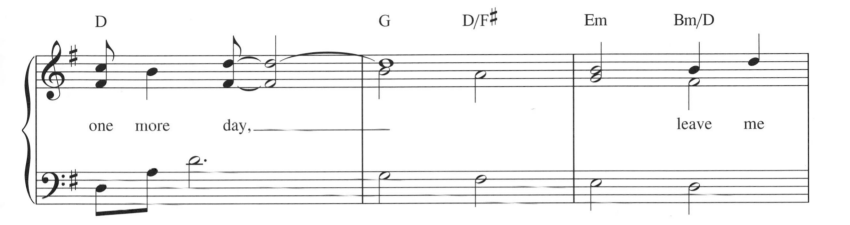

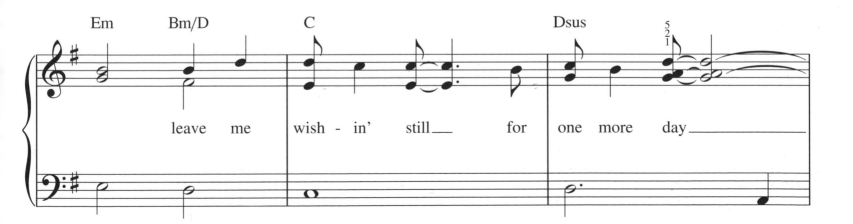

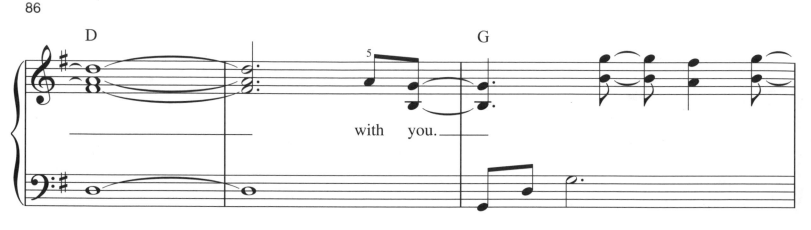

with you.

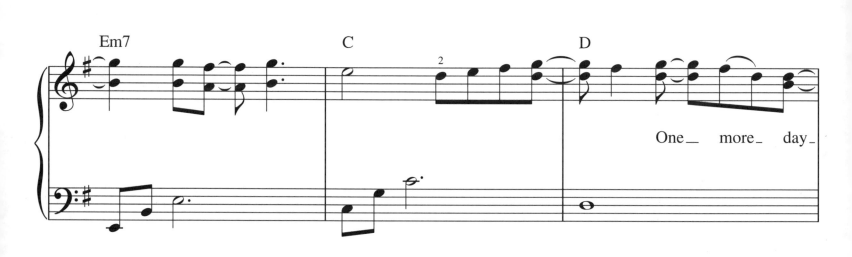

One__ more__ day__

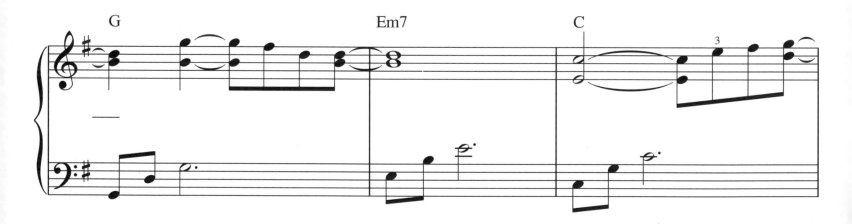

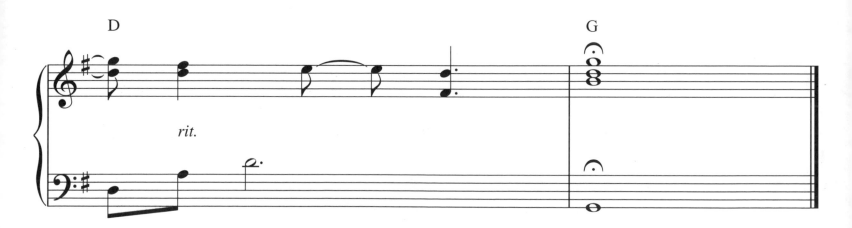

rit.

THERE YOU'LL BE

from Touchstone Pictures'/Jerry Bruckheimer Films' PEARL HARBOR

Words and Music by
DIANE WARREN

Moderately slow

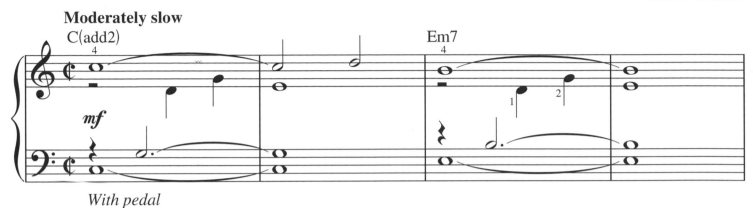

With pedal

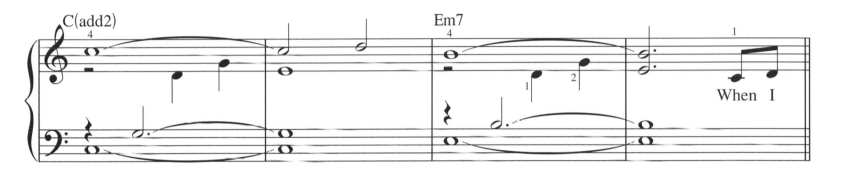

When I

think back on ___ these times ___ and the dreams we left ___ be - hind, ___
showed me how ___ it feels ___ to feel the sky with - in ___ my reach, ___

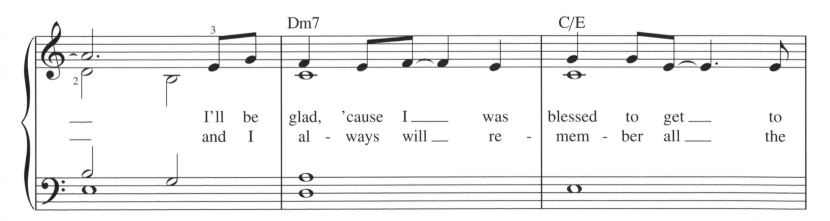

___ I'll be glad, 'cause I ___ was blessed to get ___ to
___ and I al - ways will ___ re - mem - ber all ___ the

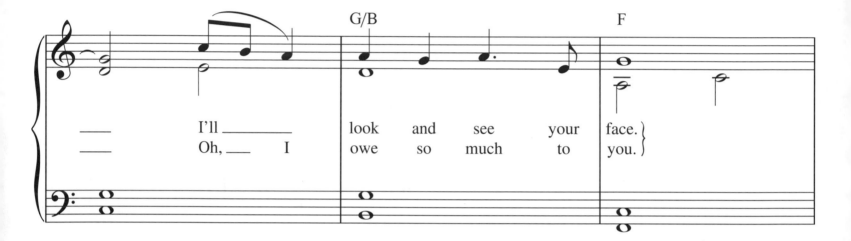

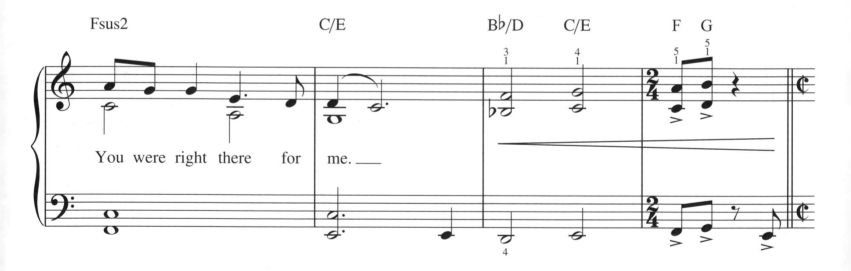

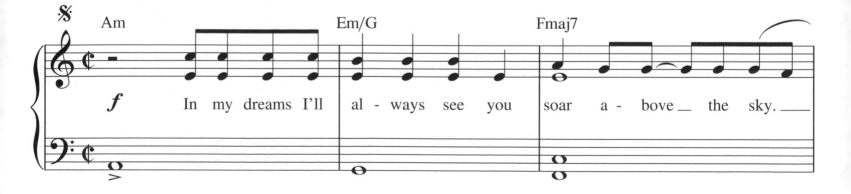

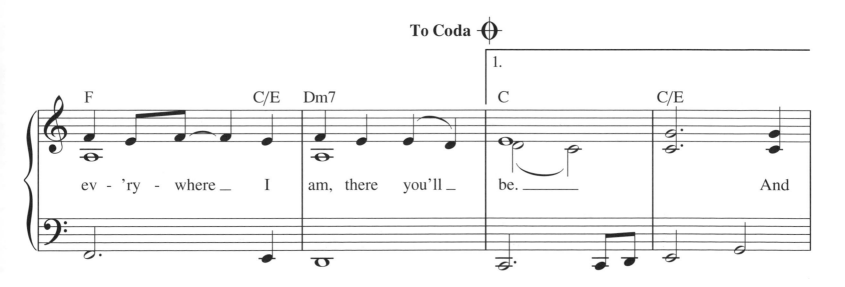

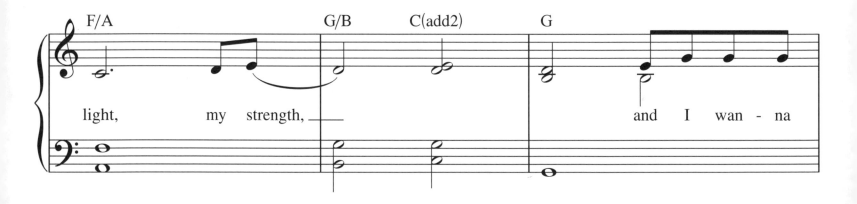

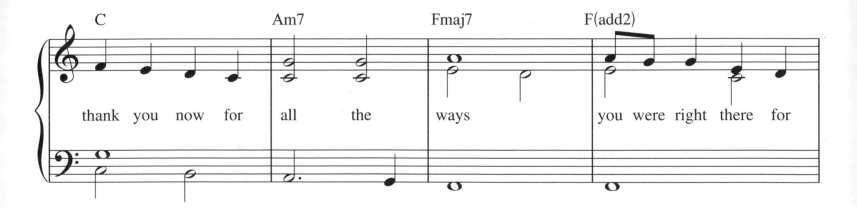

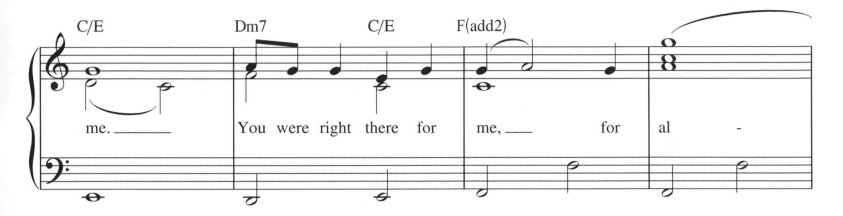

me. ____ You were right there for me, ____ for al -

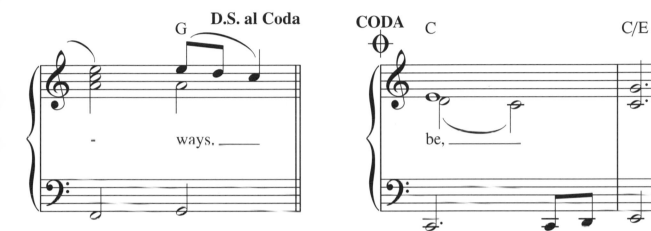

D.S. al Coda

- ways. ____

CODA

be, ____ and

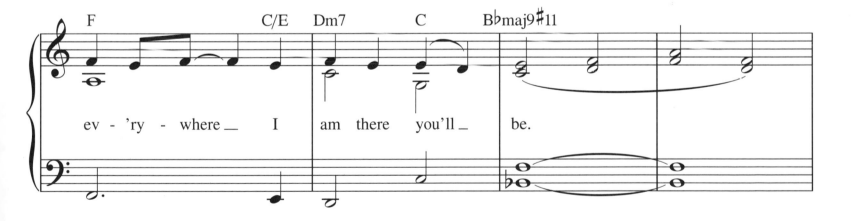

ev - 'ry - where __ I am there you'll __ be.

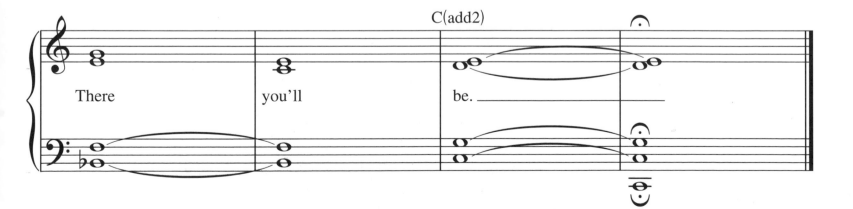

There you'll be. ____

ONLY TIME

Words and Music by ENYA,
NICKY RYAN and ROMA RYAN

De da da day. ___ De da da day. ___

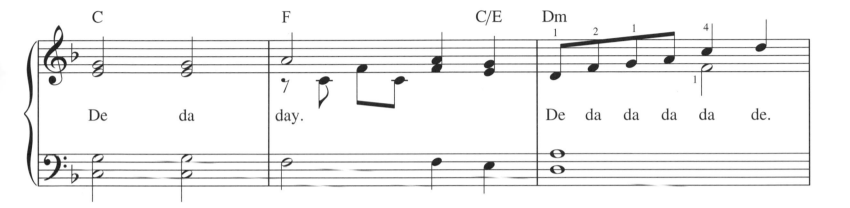

De da day. De da da da da de.

Oh ___ da day. ___ De da ___ da day ___ da day.

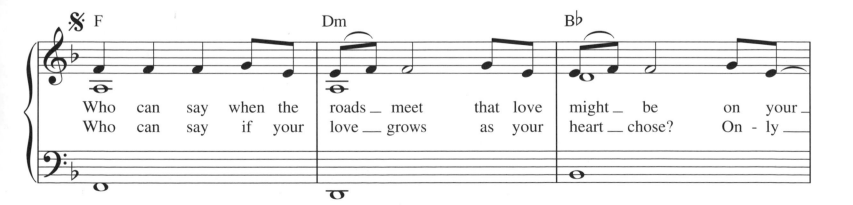

Who can say when the roads ___ meet that love might ___ be on your ___
Who can say if your love ___ grows as your heart ___ chose? On - ly ___

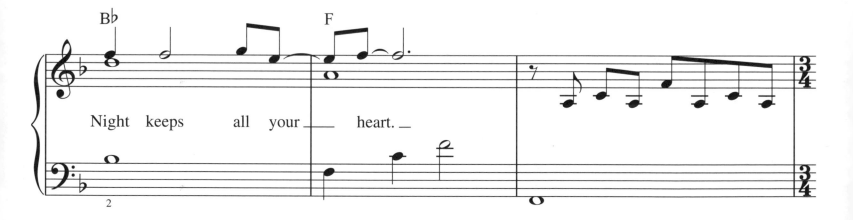

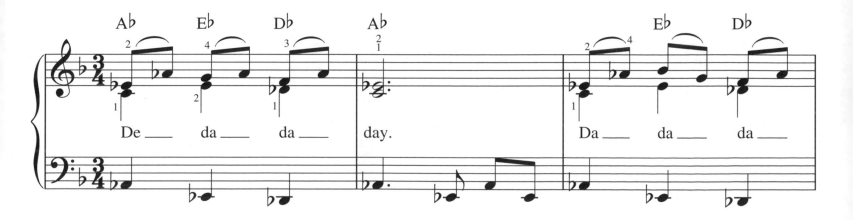

day.   De __ da __ da __ day.

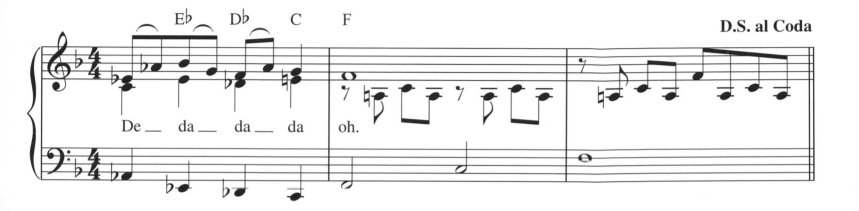

De __ da __ da __ da oh.

D.S. al Coda

CODA

Who knows?   On-ly __ time. __   Who knows?   On-ly __

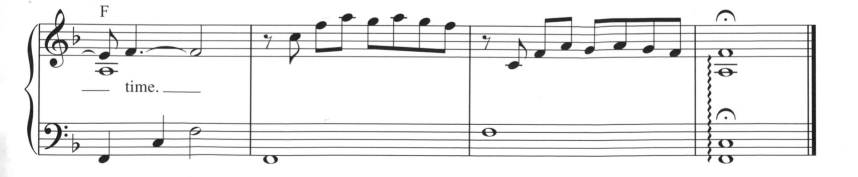

__ time. __

VALENTINE

Words and Music by JACK KUGELL
and JIM BRICKMAN

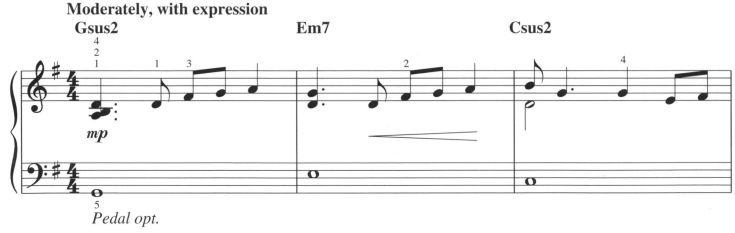

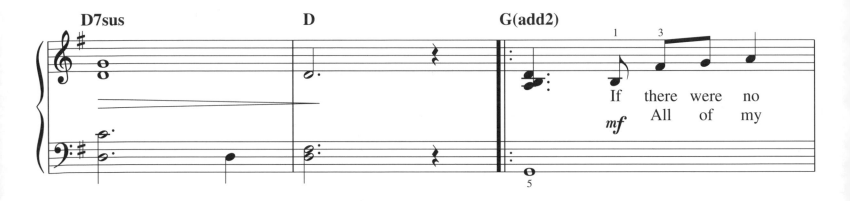

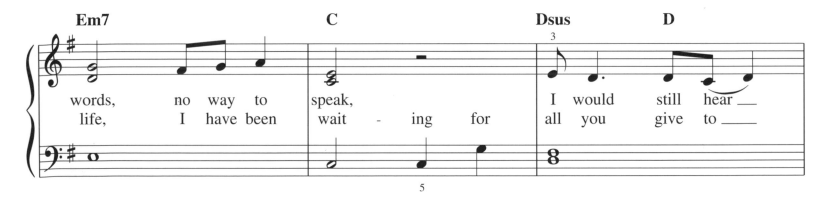

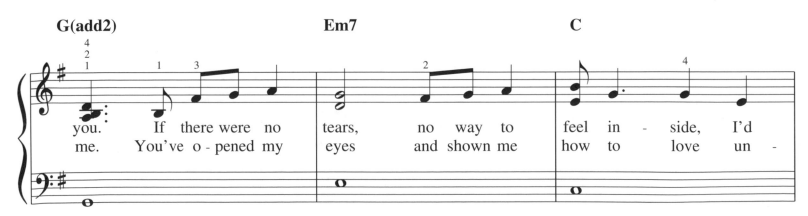

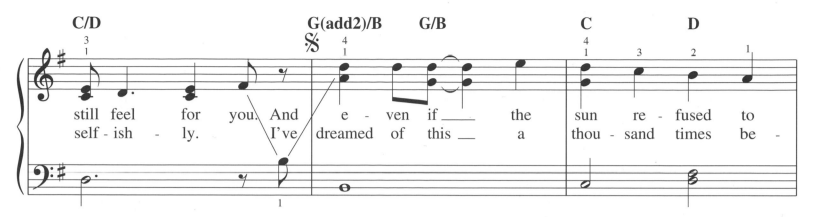

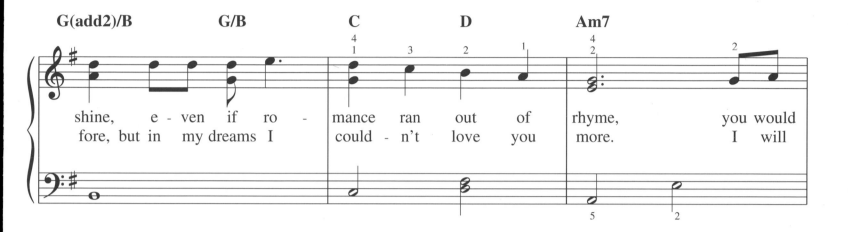

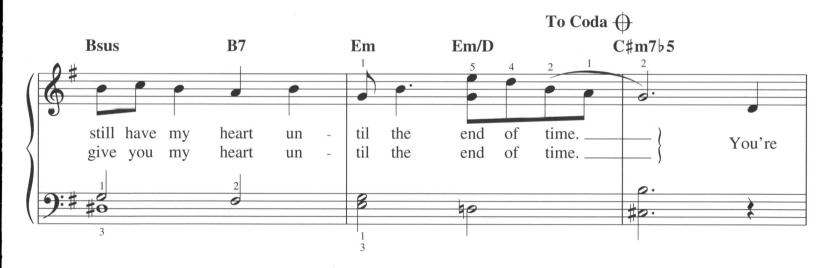

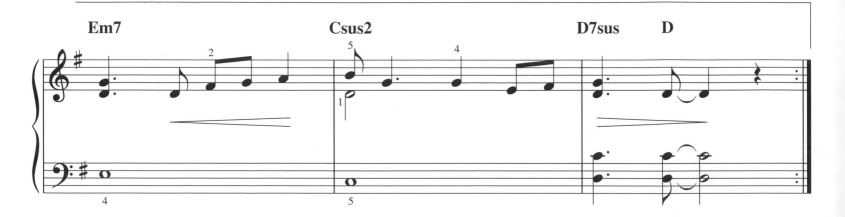

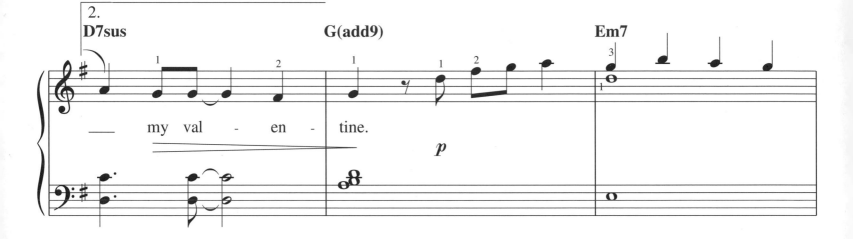

_ my val - en - tine.

La, la, la, la, la, _ la. _

And

CODA

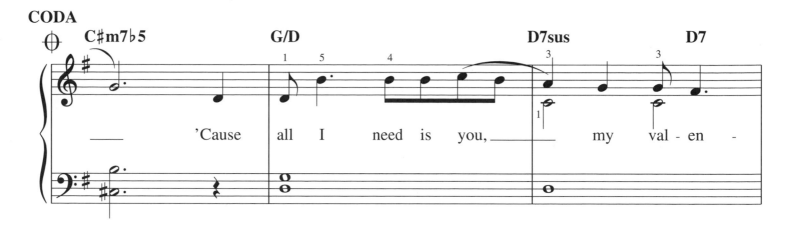

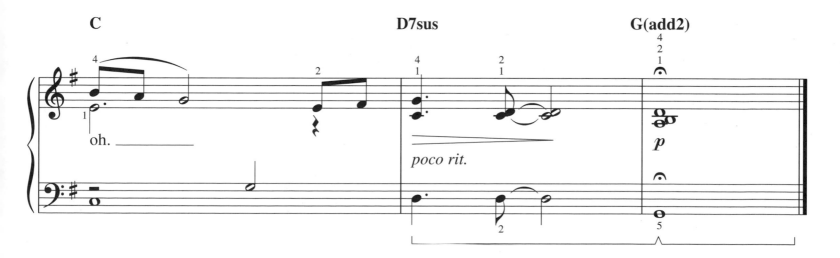

YOU HAD ME FROM HELLO

Words and Music by SKIP EWING
and KENNY CHESNEY

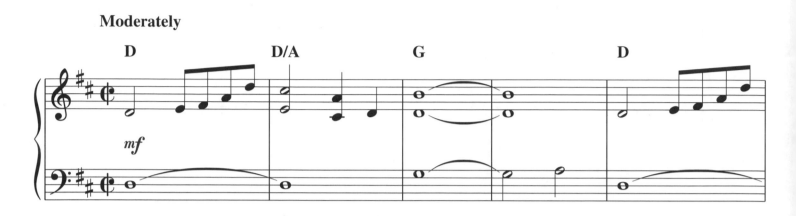

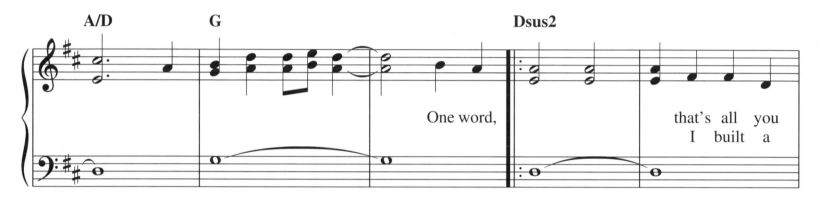

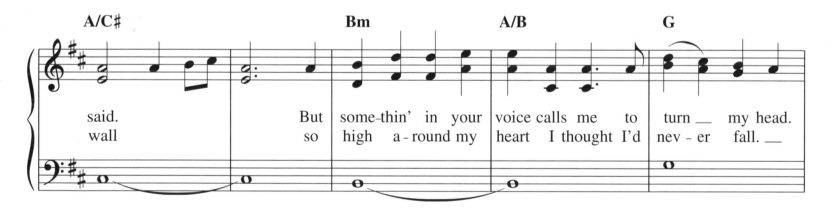

101

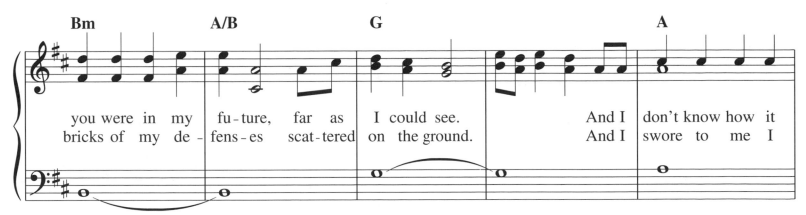

Bm   **A/B**   **G**   **A**

you were in my | fu-ture, far as | I could see. | | And I | don't know how it
bricks of my de- | fens-es scat-tered | on the ground. | | And I | swore to me I

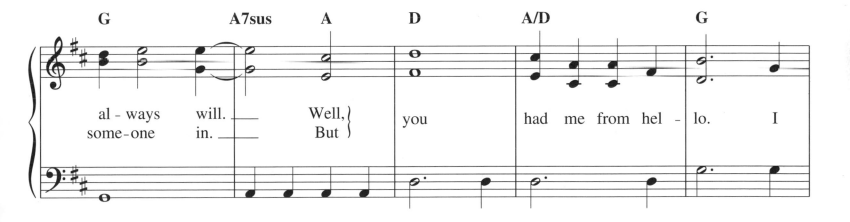

G   **D**   **Bm**

hap-pened, but it | hap-pened still. | | You | ask me if I | love you, if I
was-n't gon-na | love a-gain. | | The | last time was the | last time I let

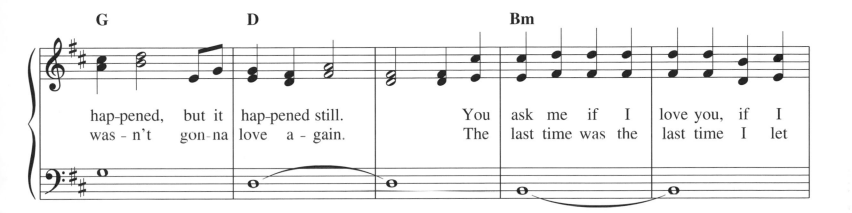

G   **A7sus**   **A**   **D**   **A/D**   **G**

al-ways will. ___ | Well, | you | had me from hel - lo. | I
some-one in. ___ | But |

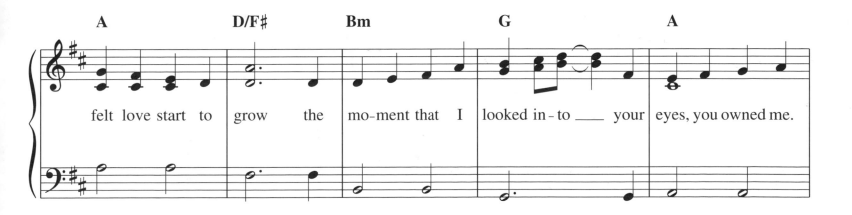

A   **D/F♯**   **Bm**   **G**   **A**

felt love start to | grow the | mo-ment that I | looked in-to ___ your | eyes, you owned me.

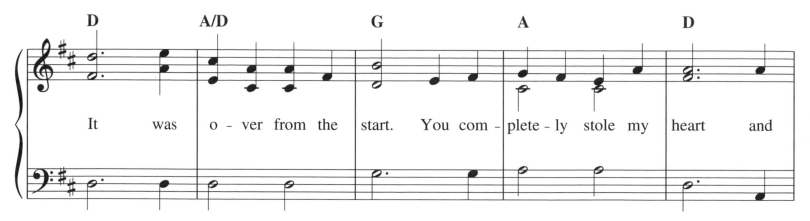

It was o - ver from the start. You com - plete - ly stole my heart and

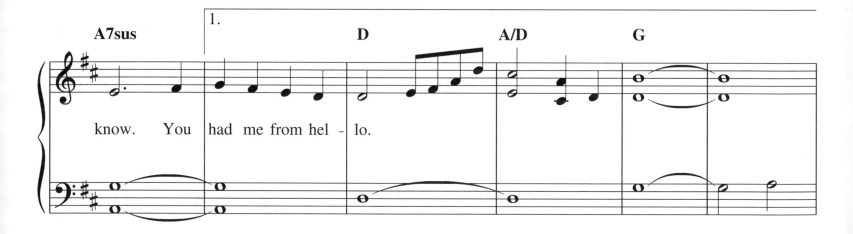

now you won't _ let go. _____ I nev - er e - ven had a chance, _ you

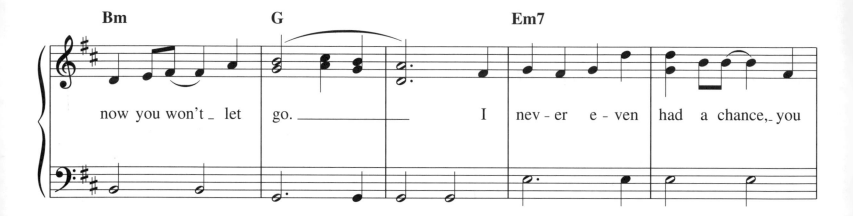

know. You had me from hel - lo.

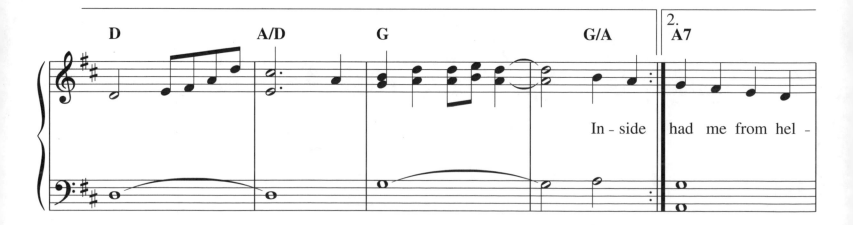

In - side had me from hel -

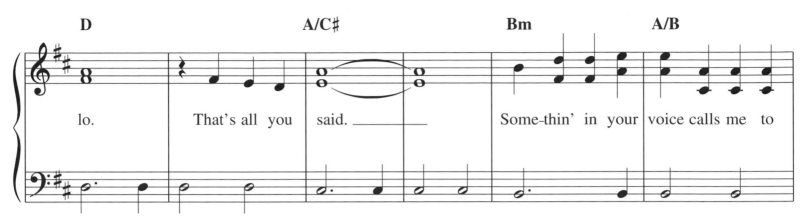

lo. That's all you said. _____ Some-thin' in your voice calls me to

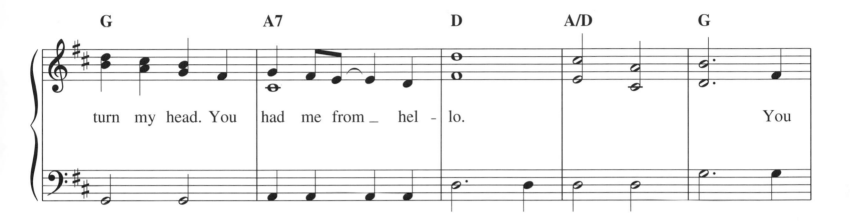

turn my head. You had me from _ hel - lo. You

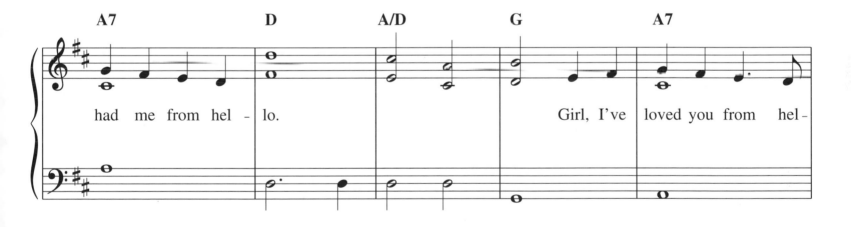

had me from hel - lo. Girl, I've loved you from hel-

lo.

WHERE WERE YOU
(When the World Stopped Turning)

Words and Music by
ALAN JACKSON

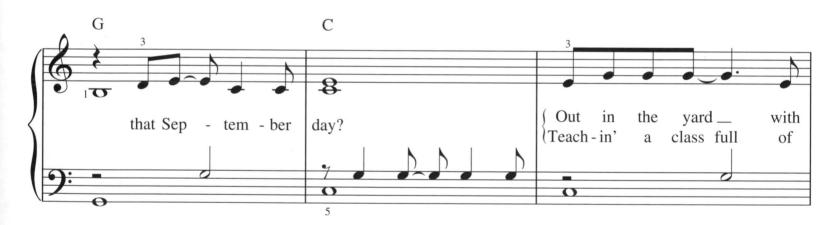

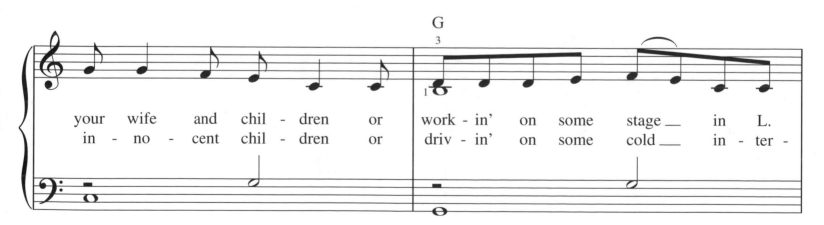

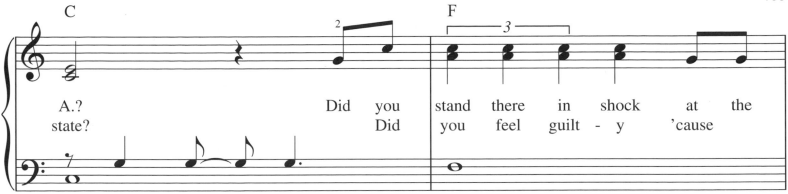

A.?
state?

Did you

stand there in shock at the
Did you feel guilt - y 'cause

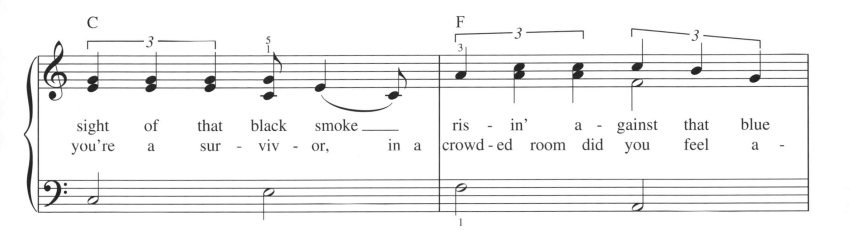

sight of that black smoke ___
you're a sur - viv - or, in a

ris - in' a - gainst that blue
crowd - ed room did you feel a -

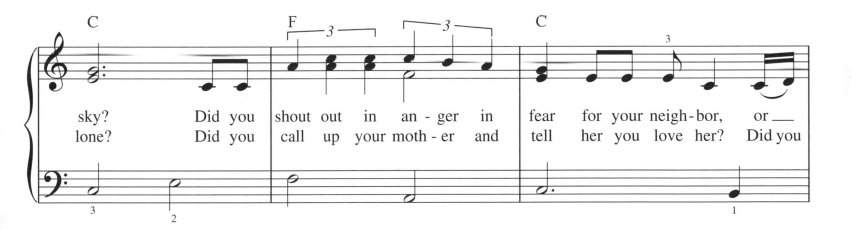

sky?
lone?

Did you
Did you

shout out in an - ger in
call up your moth - er and

fear for your neigh - bor, or ___
tell her you love her? Did you

did you just sit down and
dust off that Bi - ble at

cry?
home?

Did you
Did you

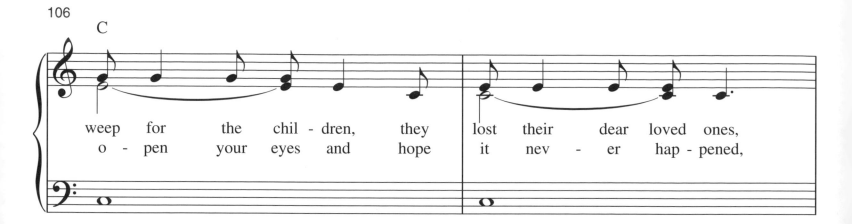

C

weep for the chil - dren, they
o - pen your eyes and hope

lost their dear loved ones,
it nev - er hap - pened,

G

C

pray for the ones who don't
close your eyes and not go to

know?
sleep?

Did you re -
Did you

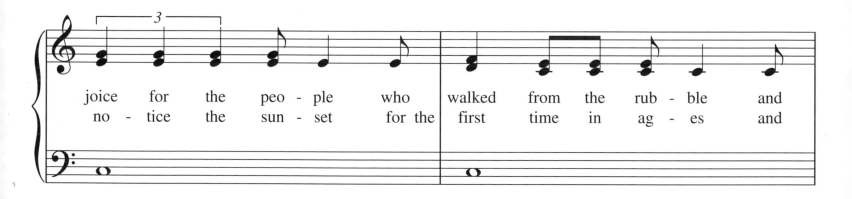

joice for the peo - ple who
no - tice the sun - set who for the

walked from the rub - ble and
first time in ag - es and

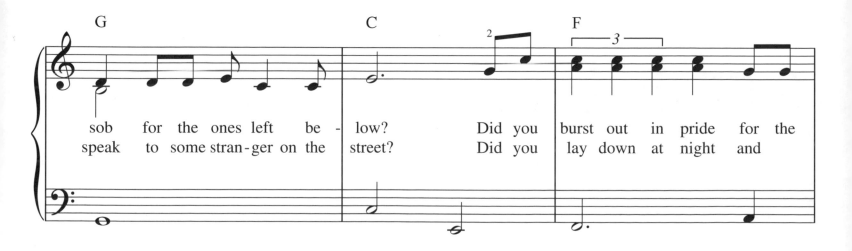

G

C

F

sob for the ones left be - low?
speak to some stran - ger on the street?

Did you
Did you

burst out in pride for the
lay down at night and

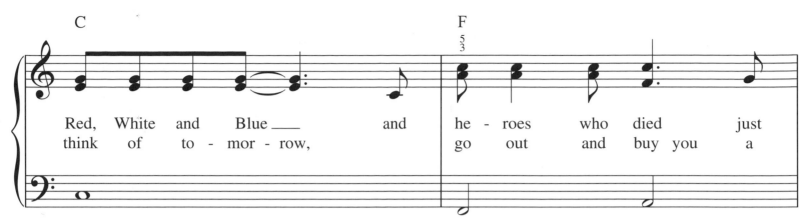

Red, White and Blue ___ and he - roes who died just
think of to - mor - row, go out and buy you a

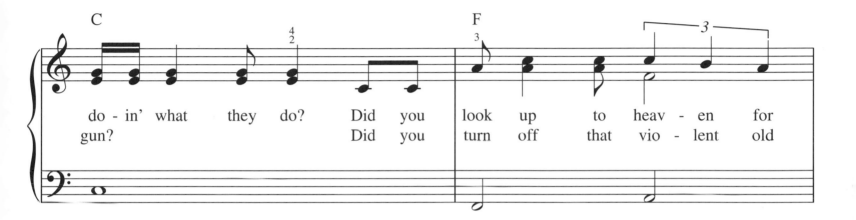

do - in' what they do? Did you look up to heav - en for
gun? Did you turn off that vio - lent old

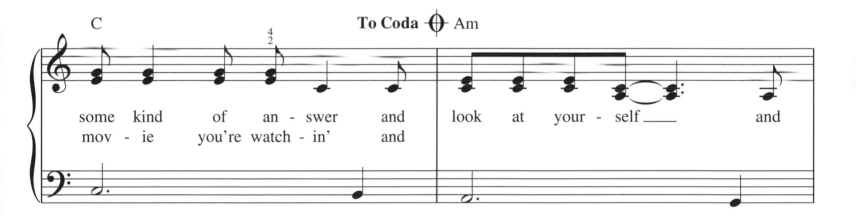

To Coda ⊕ Am

some kind of an - swer and look at your - self ___ and
mov - ie you're watch - in' and

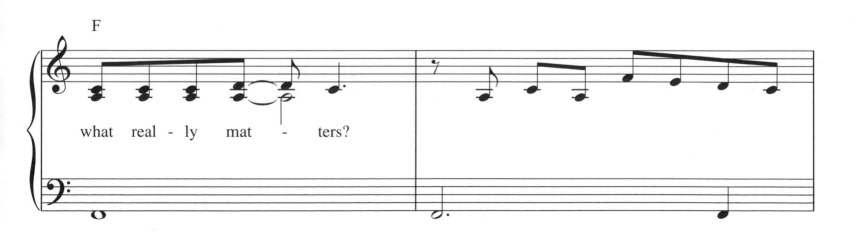

what real - ly mat - ters?

I'm just a sing-er of __ sim-ple songs. __ I'm not a real po - lit - i - cal __

man. I watch C N N, __ but I'm not __ sure I can tell you the

dif - f'rence in I - raq and I - ran. But I know Je - sus and I __

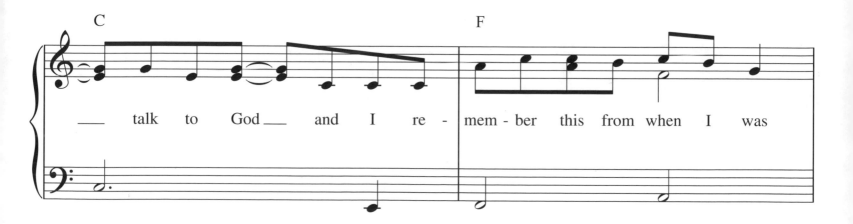

__ talk to God __ and I re - mem - ber this from when I was

young: _____ faith, hope and love are some good things He gave us

D.S. al Coda

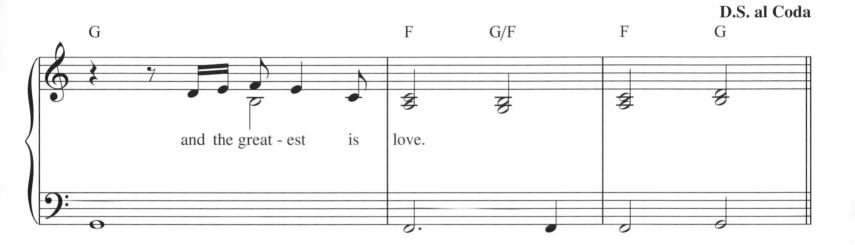

and the great-est is love.

CODA

turn on "I Love Lu - cy" re - runs? Did you go to a church ___ and hold

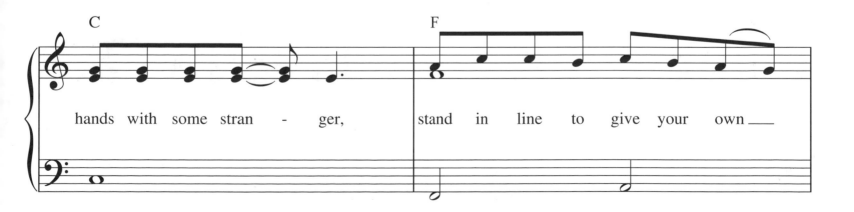

hands with some stran - ger, stand in line to give your own ___

blood? Did you just stay home __ and cling __ tight __ to your fam -'ly, thank

God you have some - bod - y to love?

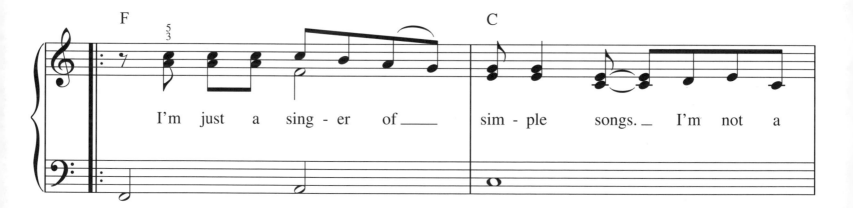

I'm just a sing - er of ____ sim - ple songs. __ I'm not a

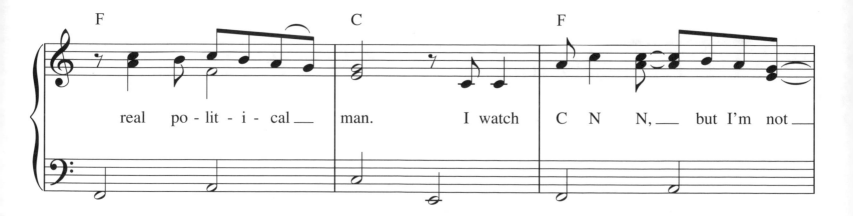

real po - lit - i - cal __ man. I watch C N N, __ but I'm not __

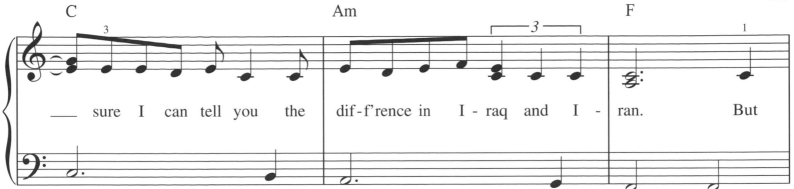

sure I can tell you the dif-f'rence in I - raq and I - ran. But

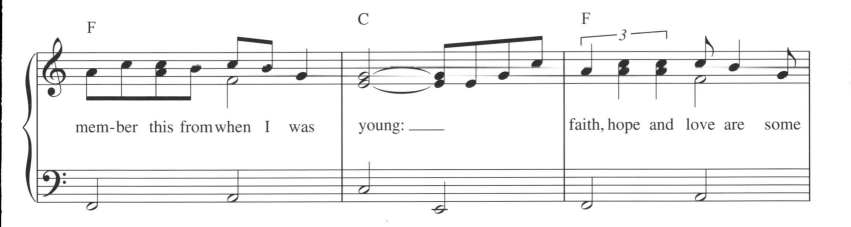

I know Je - sus and I ____ talk to God ____ and I re -

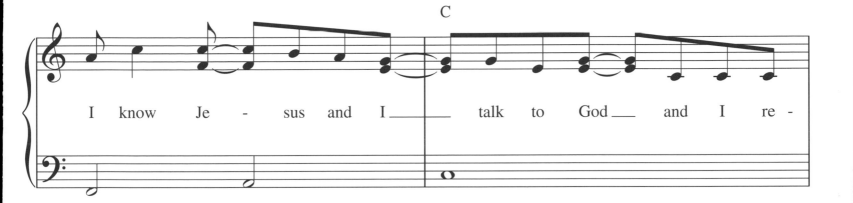

mem-ber this from when I was young: ____ faith, hope and love are some

good things He gave us and the great-est is love.

1.

love,   and the great - est   is   love,

and the great - est   is   love.

Where were   you   when   the   world____   stopped turn - in'
mp   *rit.*

that Sep - tem - ber   day? _____
p